THE CORD CEMETERY
By James Garry

History and Tombstone Inscriptions

PUBLISHED BY THE OLD DROGHEDA SOCIETY©
PRINTED BY NORTH EAST PRINTERS LTD. 1999

The Cord Cemetery

FOREWORD

In Holyhood Cemetery, Boston, lie the remains of Dowth born Fenian, Orator, Poet and Freeman, John Boyle O'Reilly. Buried also in Holyhood, is Patrick A. Collins, the first Irish Mayor of Boston, and Joseph Kennedy, father of the American political dynasty. There is no order to the burials in the graveyard, and so it is necessary to search stone by stone, if one is carrying out genealogical or historical research.

Here in Drogheda, the equivalent of Holyhood is the Cord Cemetery, where many of the prominent citizens of Drogheda's past are now buried; John Mangan, a Mayor and noted nationalist, John Sheil, the poet, and the 'notorious Leinster Highwayman' Michael Collier, to name but a few. The cemetery is in a poor condition however, when compared to its Bostonian counterpart. No manicured lawns or trimmed trees, here, broken headstones and overgrown weeds have become the order of the day.

The publication of James Garry's 'Cord Cemetery' will now make it easy for the researcher, to check on those buried in the graveyard. This book is a valuable asset to the written history of Drogheda. The historian will no longer have to search from stone to stone, seeking information, as James, is his usual meticulous manner, has carefully recorded it all.

With luck the publication of this book will give the impetus needed to all denominations, Corporations, Parishes and other interested groups, to come together and endeavour to restore the Cord Cemetery to its former glory, with Bostonian like manicuried lawns, as neat as the columns in this book, where the townspeople can go and recall their dead generations.

Sean Collins.

Hon. Chairman,

Old Drogheda Society.

June 1999

THE CORD CEMETERY, DROGHEDA
By James Garry

Origins

The Priory of St Laurence – a foundation of the Crutched Friars – was founded and built by the Mayor and Burgesses of the town, on this site, the Cord Road/Thomas Street area of the town. To this Priory was attached burial ground, now known as the Cord, as D'Alton writes, 'finely situated overlooking the Boyne and planted with evergreens' he, in his researches, when he was compiling the 'History of Drogheda' in 1844, failed in unearthing very little of its history. However it is on record that in 1310, its Prior had royal letters of protection, and in 1441 John Davis, then its principal, granted bed and clothing in said house to John Clonnegan, for the terms of his natural life.

OCTAVIAN de PLACIO

Dowling in his annuals, refers to the year 1493, the trial of an ecclesiastical cause, somewhat connected with this house, where Octavian de Palacio, then Archbishop of Armagh, asserted his rights of paramount primacy. A case had been pending between the Bishop of Leighlin and his own Dean and Chapter; the latter appealed the Metropolitan jurisdiction of Dublin, but, not obtaining relief there, advanced their appeal to the court of Armagh, when Octavian cited their opponents to appear before himself at the House and Chancel of St. Lawerence, near Drogheda, within the octave of St. Patrick; but the further course of the proceedings does not appear.

EXTENSIVE PROPERTIES

The Priory of St. Laurence, like all other religious houses, was dis-solved under Henry VIII in 1547. The last Prior, Stephen Roche, was seized under the site, comprising a stone church, covered with tiles; a kitchen and two stables thatched; a cowhouse, barn and kiln, two parks of half an acre each, planted with ash trees. An orchard of half an acre and a stang: twenty acres of pasture, one and a half of meadow near Philipstown, twelve of pasture and of meadow near Woddsland, half an acre of pasture in Talbot's Park, with another acre adjoining; twenty acres of pasture on the west side of the highway leading to the Commons, fourteen acres of land called Hookeland, adjacent to Bathe's highway; half an acre of pasture in Our Lady's land, on the east side of the highway; two acres of Meadow in Cloneralthe.

HORSE & WATER MILLS

A park of Brushwood with an acre of pasture on the north of the lord of Howth, two acres of pasture, south of the said lord; fifteen acres of pasture, called Trym's Field; two acres of pasture, east of said lord, a water mill, five acres, east of the Lady's land, four acres called Mort Park, lying on both sides of the land of Thomas St., Laurence; an acre north of the Mort Park, the horse mill park-four acres, an acre of pasture called the Commons, Seeroge's Park, an acre and a half, two acres on St James', half an acre of ash, a messuage in St. Sunday's Street, a messuage near the pillory(Peter St), another in Fish Street, a third in Dyer Street, a common of two acres of pasture and bushes near Plunkett's Land, and three acres and a half in said common, near the Newtown; all of which possessions were likewise granted to the Corporation of Drogheda, almost 120 acres with outhouses, buildings and mills.

CORPORATION GRANTS

The Corporation in turn, granted, 'St Laurence Mill' in 1669 to Alderman Thomas Dixon, for sixty one years, at the annual rent of thirty shillings; and in 1700, Alderman William Elwood obtained from them, a more distinct conveyance of 'St Laurence's Hospital, lying outside St Laurence Gate', with the haggard, garden, orchard, church and churchyard at the yearly rent of £3-16-1d. The premises were in 1760, demised to John Graham, Junior.

The Cord Cemetery

EARLIEST STONE

Despite all the property dispersal's, the church yard was in use and the earliest burial that we know of, is the broken piece, with the date '24 Nov 1613' now lying beside the ruined gable of the church, and over seventy interments are recorded up to 1799. Down through the following century, many illustrious citizens' of the town were interred. Among them the Dominican, Rev. Thomas Burke, founder of the Drogheda School of the Harpers in 1843.

NUNS BURIAL PLACE

The burial place of the Sienna Nuns was denoted by a stone bearing the date 1792. This was not seen until the remains were exhumed in 1972 and translated to their own graveyard, at the rear of the convent in the Cord Road. The Sisters of Charity did likewise and took the remains of eight nuns to St. Peter's Cemetery, 8th August 1980.

ACROSTIC EPITAPH

Several fine family monuments are to be seen; the Chesters 1708; Gernons, Colemans and Peter Roe 1739. The Richard Archbold stone is missing. He was a distinguished solicitor and the first Catholic who qualified for admission to that profession, according to the Act. An acrostic epitaph to James McDonnell, and still to be seen on his headstone, was composed by his daughter, Eliza, afterwards Mrs Devin. The McDonnells were the descendants of an old, highly respected, and most charitable Drogheda family who held large estate in the town. Amongst other possessions, the McDonnells owned the large orchard, which the Christian Brothers bought in 1866, from Mrs Devin, when they were contemplating building the existing convent at Sunday's Gate.

ARCHBISHOP'S GRAVE

There is no distinguishing mark, or any sign, denoting the grave of Dr Bryan O'Reilly, Archbishop of Armagh, who was interred here about the year 1757, having died at Termonfeckin, where in a small farmhouse, he resided during the chief period of his prelacy.

The overgrown condition of the Cemetery from Thomas Street.

'SHEIL THE POET'

Buried in the Cord are the remains of the poet John Sheil, who wrote his own acrostic epitaph and hoped to have it inscribed on his tomb. However like Robert Emmet's, Sheil's epitaph was never written on any stone. Born in the north of Ireland, he came with his parents, to reside in Drogheda, some say at the Greenlanes, others, the Marsh Road. This was in 1798 and young Sheil remembered and retained lively recollections of this stirring period and the insurrectionary movements of Lord Edward Fitzgerald and Robert Emmet. Mr Hugh Caraher, a native of Drogheda, residing then in north of Wales, wrote a series of articles for the Argus, under the caption 'The Men of Other Days', a writing of the poetic efforts of Sheil said:

> *"What Beranger was to the peasantry of France, Sheil was in a better sense to the faithful peasantry of Ireland"*

His love songs were popular in rural districts, 'Letty Lee' being quite a reigning favourite. Sheil died in 1872 and his funeral expenses were paid by the proprietor of the Argus, John Hughes. Here is the un-inscribed acrostic epitaph as written by him:

J udicious reader, stand and muse awhile;
O ne moment pause, perhaps I might make you feel;
H ere interred beneath this mortal soil,
N o King or Prince, but humble little Sheil.

S weet Erin, dear, in rustic homely verse,
H e mourned her wrongs, and shouted forth her praise.
E xtollled her sons, her creed, her lovely crest;
I mpressed that maxim all his mortal days,
L ord granted his soul perpetual rest and peace.

Other songs by Sheil are taken from a booklet found in the 1950's all pertaining to local areas: 'Mary the Star of Culfore'; 'The Nice Little Neat Little Factory Maid'; 'Garristown Jack'; 'The Brilliant Bright Torch of Ardee'; 'Young Henry Sweet Ravansdale'; 'The Flower of Beamore'; 'Bellewstown Hill'; 'Shady Groves of Sweet Ardee':

THE BELLEWSTOWN HILL

(From 'The Humour of Ireland', Walter Scott Ltd., London Published 1898).

If a respite ye'd borrow from turmoil or sorrow,
I'll tell you the secret of how it is done,
T'is found in this statement of all the excitement
That Bellewstown know when the races come on.
Make one of the party whose spirits are hearty,
Get a seat on a trap that is safe not to spill,
In its well pack a hamper, then offer for a scamper,
And huroo for the glories of Bellewstown Hill!

On, the road how they dask on, rank, beauty, and fashion,
Banagher bangs , by the table o'war!
From the coach of the quality, down to the jollity
Jogging along on an ould jaunting car.
Though straw cushions are placed, two feet thick at laste,
It's jigging and jum ' ig mollify still;
Oh, the cheeks of my Nelly are shaking like jelly,
From the jolting she gets as she jogs to the Hill.
In the thetes play the pipers, the fiddlers and fifers.
Those rollicking lilts such as Ireland best knows;
While Paddy is prancing, his colleen is dancing,
Demure, with her eyes quite intent on her toes.
More power to you Micky! Faith your feet isn't Sticky,
But hounds from the boards like a pea from a quill.

Oh, t'would cure a rheumatic – he'd jump up esctatic,
At 'Tatler Jack Walsh' upon Bellestown Hill.
Oh, 'tis there 'neath the haycocks, all splendid like paycocks.
In chattering groups that the quality dine,
Sitting cross legged like tailors, the gentlemen dealers
In chattering groups and come out mighty fine.
And the gentry from Navan and Cavan are 'having'
Neath the shade of the trees, an Arcadian quadrille
All we read in the pages of pastoral ages
Tell of no scene like this upon Bellewstown Hill.

Arrive at the summit, the view that you come at,
From etherealised Mourne to Tara ascends,
There's no scene in our sireland, dear Ireland, old Ireland.
To which nature more exquisite loveliness lends.
And the soil 'neath your feet has a memory sweet,
The patriots deeds they hallow it still;
Eighty-two volunteers(would today saw their peers!)
Marched past in review upon Bellewstown Hill.

But hark! There's a shout – the horses are out –
'Long the ropes, on the stand, what a hullaballoo!
To old Crock-a-Fatha, the people dot the route
Broad plateau around are all for a view.
"Come, Ned, my thigh fellow, I'll bet on the yellow!
Success to the green! Faith, we'll stand by it still!"
The uplands and hollows they're skimming like swallows,
Till they flash by the post upon Bellewstown Hill.

"COLLIER THE ROBBER" (1780-1849)

While few people know that the Cord is the last-,resting place of Michael Collier, the "Last of the Irish Highwaymen", fewer still are aware that his burial took place by candlelight. It was Patrick (Pa) Moonan, a stone cutter, Pearse Park, Drogheda (d.1975) who first pointed out the only mark in the graveyard showing the spot where the highwayman is buried. It is a chunk of roughly cut limestone standing at an acute angle. It bears no inscription of any kind, but Mr. Moonan said...... "It is definitely the grave of Collier, my grandfather told me this."

As a highwayman, Collier operated on the roads of Louth, Meath, Cavan and north Dublin. His most daring robbery was a hold-up of the Dublin-Belfast mail coach at "Bloody Hollow" between Drumcondra and Swords. Other daring escapades followed until Collier was captured by the military, tried and sentenced in Trim. No proof of murder could be found against him, so instead of hanging, his sentence was transportation to the penal colony of Botany Bay. Here his career took an unexpected turn.

Soon he was released again: He joined a Colonial Regiment of the English army. And before long, Private Michael Collier was promoted, given a free discharge and his passage paid back to Ireland.

He settled down in Ludlow Street, Navan. There, he kept open house for any man on the run, but it was noticed that any man who availed of his shelter was soon captured by the military. The truth is that Collier was now a secret agent - in the pay of Dublin Castle. Ireland was then in an acute state of discontent, with the Young Ireland Association planning its Rebellion in 1848.

Some years later this last part of Collier's career was unearthed by a neighbour of his in Navan. W.F. Wakeman. MRIA. the historian, who lived a few doors away from him. Wakeman often wondered how Collier lived, for he had no visible livelihood, yet he always had plenty of money.

Wakeman saw an account book of the Inspector of the R.I.C. in County Meath, and in it he found mysterious entries like these; "Paid to C for secret information, £1," and again "Paid to C, for information £1-15-0d" The Inspector confirmed that this indeed were payments made to Collier.

His days as a spy were not to last long. In 1849 he came to Drogheda on his way to Bellewstown Races, a town where the dreaded disease of Cholera was now raging. He entered the house of Mr. Edward Reilly, at 86 West Street, and after some time he complained of being unwell. Not withstanding the dangerous character of the disease, Reilly put him to bed and Drs. Ellis and Darbey were called in. Both these gentlemen pronounced it a case of Asiatic Cholera.

Despite the application of every remedy, Collier breathed his last at 10.30 o'clock on the evening of 13th August 1849. His body was taken on a cart, to the Cord, followed only by six individuals – Messers. B.Reilly , Thomas Rowe, - Johnson, Hugh O'Neill, William Reynolds and James Fitzpatrick, and by the light of candle, his grave was dug and this man , who filled so large a space in the history of Lenister, was laid in a humble grave, with no marker.

The Cord Cemetery

An artist's impression of 'Collier the Robber' courtesy of John McHale.

Mr. Patrick Moonan points out the stone marking the grave of 'Collier the Robber' in the Cord Cemetery.

ERECTED BY PUBLIC SUBSCRIPTION

Two monuments in the Cord were erected by the people of Drogheda, at two different periods in the town's history. They are the only headstones bear the inscription "Erected by Public Subscription".

THOMAS GULSHEY... A tall pinnacle on a plinth, was erected in 1842, to Mr.Thomas Gulshey, as a tribute to his "great zeal and efficiency" as Secretary of the Burial Committee. He died on 6th January 1841 at the age of 70 years. The amount subscribed for this monument was £15-18-9d, and it was disbursed as follows : 6s-9d to James Denneny for carting nine loads of stone; Michael Donnelly, labourer, 2s-4d; John Devin, ma n, 5s; Thomas Hammond, Sheephouse, for the cut stone, £15; the balance, 4s-8d went to the cemetery fund.

JAMES WOODS A simple Celtic cross on a base, is the second monument by "public subscription", erected to James Woods, who was "shot by one of the military on St. Mary's Bridge" on 20th November 1868. The election of an M.P. for Drogheda was taking place in the Tholsel. The candidates were Benjamin Whitworth, Leopold McClintock and Francis Brodigan. A detachment of the 9th Regiment of Foot, under a Captain Knox, in company with some troopers of the 14th Hussars, was escorting a party of, conservative voters from the railway station, to the voting booth at the Tholsel. As they crossed St.Mary's Bridge, they were attacked by a mob of some 1,500 to 2,000 strong, who threw stones, sticks and bottles at the party and some hand-to-hand fighting ensued.

Four officers and fourteen men were injured, some severely, and the Riot Act was read a number of times. The officer in command of the escort was knocked out by a stone, and while he was incapacitated, two soldiers opened fire without orders, killing one civilian ... At the subsequent inquest the coroner's jury returned a verdict of manslaughter, against one of the two privates, but could not say which. Some time later the two men were tried for murder, in Dublin, but were acquitted for lack of definite evidence as to which had fired the fatal shot.

The dead civilian was James Woods, a worker in Chadwick's Mill on the Marsh Road. After death was pronounced, the body was taken to a house in one of the courts in Peter Street, where it was waked

Receipt for Grave in the Cord. 'No. 63 Cord Burial Committee. Received from Mrs. Patk Magrath of Newtown, Co. Meath, the sum of Two Pounds Ten Shillings for Grave, along east wall in the Cord Burial Ground. Patk Byrne, Hon. Treasurer, Drogheda this 10th day of April 1889'. (Courtesy: Margaret Startup.)

THE FUNERAL OF JAMES WOODS

The *Drogheda Argus*, 28th November, 1868, has the following description of the Woods funeral.

"On Sunday last the funeral of James Woods who met his death from a bullet fired by a soldier of the 9th Foot. took place, and was one of the largest and most impressive funeral demonstrations that Drogheda ever witnessed."

"On the afternoon of Saturday last placards were posted in different parts of the town announcing that the burial would take place at half past one o'clock on Sunday and proceed through the principal streets of the town. From one o'clock crowds began to assemble near the Tholsel and in Peter Street, the locality in which deceased was waked, and shortly after the appointed hour there were 8,000 to 10,000 persons present."

"In Fair Street were marshalled those who intended to form front ranks consisting of about 150 members of a tontine society to which deceased belonged. These were placed two by two each wearing a black scarf and hat band with a rosette on his breast."

"Next came about 1500 young men in marching order ten deep, all respectably dressed, and each wearing a green ribbon around his hat or a green rosette in his dress. This part of the procession attracted much attention the young men being so well organised."

"At a quarter to two a four horse hearse was drawn up to receive the coffin, but the people preferred to carry it on the shoulders and the procession commenced to move in Fair Street."

"In the rear of the young men, described above, followed one immense crowd of men, women, and boys, the greater portion of them being from the rural parts, and next were about 800 persons eight deep, of the trades and working classes all of whom were decently clad, and each exhibiting a green badge of some sort, but more particularly crape hat-bands tied with green ribbons."

"Next followed from 600 to 800 boys in rank and file, men with green scarf's and white rods, being stationed outside the ranks to keep the juveniles in order. The hearse was next followed by a vast number of shop keepers and traders and then another batch of 500 men displaying green ribbons or laurel wreaths."

"These were succeeded by nearly one thousand young women all neatly attired and each exhibiting a profusion of ribbons of the national colour which flaunted behind from their head-dress. The fair processionists walked six deep observing the utmost order and decorum."

"Immediately after the coffin came in view borne on the shoulders of four men. The following clergymen followed the remains; the venerable Archdeacon Tierney, P.P.,
Rev. James,Powderly, C.C.,
Rev. H. McKee, C.C.,
Rev. P. V. Meadthe, O.P.,
Rev. Dr. Murphy, O.P.,
Rev. F. Doyle, O.S.A.,
Rev. Mr. Chambers O.S.A.,
Rev. Thomas Murphy, P.P. St. Peters.

Rev. T. Matthews, P.P., V.F. St. Mary's,
Rev. Mr. Kavanagh, O.S.F.
Several of our magistrates and members of the Civil Boards, professional gentlemen, Town Councillors, shopkeepers and other respectable citizens also walked.

The Rear was brought up by a large concourse of people of both sexes belonging to the town and rural districts. A large number of the Constabulary was present but it must be observed that a more orderly assemblage there could not be. There was a total absence of any disorder and the peace of the town was altogether undisturbed from beginning to end. There could not have been less than 15,000 persons in all."

The procession passed through Fair Street, Great George Street, West Street, Laurence Street, Laurence Gate and on to the Cord Burial Ground. The burial service having been read and the grave closed, the dense assemblage slowly and peacefully returned into town"

"The deceased filled the office of time-keeper at Mr Chadwicks Mill on the Marsh, was a native of Dundalk and an orphan. He was 22 years of age and bore a character for sobriety, good conduct and in offensiveness.

"It is proposed to raise a monument over the grave to commemorate the circumstances under which Woods lost his life. A numerously attended meeting was held in the Sheriffs Room in the Mayoralty House on Monday afternoon in furtherance of the object and practical steps were taken to carry it out by the appointment of a committee, district collectors and a treasurer. A meeting was later held and the committee earnestly requested those who desire to subscribe to the fund to forward the amount of their subscriptions to the treasurer or secretary. A large sum has already been subscribed. Mr. Hughes proprietor of this newspaper has been named as treasurer and Mr. Peter Johnson, ever active in a patriotic and good cause is secretary to the fund."

On the previous Saturday, the inquest on Woods was held in the Tholsel. There was some difficulty in getting a jury as some had not attended the summons. The Coroner with Dr. Kelly Fair Street left the inquest to view the body where it was laid in a house in one of the courts in Peter Street.

Evidence of identification was given by Patrick McGuinness of Patrick Street, who said: "I am a flax-dresser, 1 knew the deceased James Woods for about two years; He was a clerk and ticket marker in the Marsh Mill."

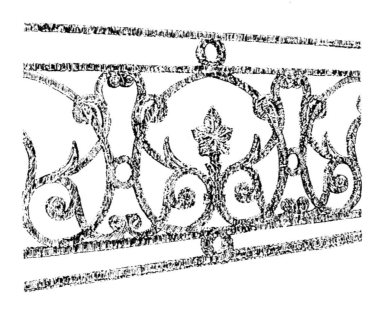

THE MORTUARY CHAPEL

The Mortuary Chapel in 1975.

In 1872 a committee was formed for the purpose of erecting a chapel in the Cord; headed by Canon Cosson, PP, it consisted of Fr.Moonan, John Chadwick, JP, F.Chadwick, E.McDonough, John Hughes, Patrick Byrne, John Kelly, Captain Branigan, P.Reilly, John F.Greene and Owen McEnteggart. Designed by P.J.Dodd, the chapel was erected by contractor Thomas Butterly. It was described by the local press (*Drogheda Argus*, 27th June 1874) as follows ..."Completed in comparatively short time, considering the many calls that Catholic munificence had responded to. It is a handsome cut stone structure, simple in design, but adapted to its purpose. It is beautifully finished inside and out, with stained glass window, handsome altar, polished seats, and externally with pointed roof and dwarf spire, surmounted by the cross." Placed just inside the entrance to the burial ground, the chapel fills the view at once, with fine effect and is not only beautifying to the grounds where it is erected, but is also a prominent improvement to the locality."...

The consecration of the mortuary chapel took place on Sunday 21st June 1874. His Grace, Most Rev. Dr.McCettigan, Archbishop of Armagh, was attended by the following. Very Rev. Archdeacon Gosson, PP, Very Rev. M.A.Cavanagh, O.S.F., cross bearer; Fr. Meadthe,OP; Fr. McKee,PP; Rev. T.Murphy and Rev. J.Moonan, curates of St. Peter's; Rev. J.Coleman, OSA; and J.Cooney, OSF. The consecration was gone through in strict conformity with the ritual; then Mass was celebrated by Father Moonan, and afterwards His Grace the Primate, preached in the open air, a plain but most impressive discourse from a dais erected at the end of the chapel, his attentive audience in a wide circle standing around in the graveyard.

The vaults underneath the chapel extend the full length and breath of the building and the remains deposited there, are dealt within a separate section of the Study. The first funeral Mass held in the new chapel was that of Miss Eliza Kennedy, North Quay. Mass was celebrated in the chapel, every first Monday morning, in the month, at 9 o'clock, for the repose of the souls of those interred in the Cord, right up to the late 1940s, when it was discontinued. The chapel was leased, as a clubroom, to the Drogheda Branch of the Red Cross, by Right Rev. Monsignor Henry Laverty, PP,VG, St.Peter's, on 31st October 1974.

EXTENTION

The eastern wing of the cemetery was extended, and a new entrance in Thomas Street, was built in 1826. Formerly, the entrance was in the Cord Road, between Thomas and Cord Terrace. A further extension took place 1838, as is recorded on a stone plaque beside the gate. "A portion of this Burial Ground, containing 1 rood and 26 perches, was given, a free gift, to the inhabitants, by the Corporation, in the year 1838."

SIGNS OF OVERCROWDING

Used continually down through the years, it is not surprising that in 1880, the overcrowded condition of the burial ground was causing concern. The first reference to the overcrowding, was raised by

Alderman Daly, JP. at a Corporation meeting in March 1885, who asked for a further extension of the ground. He said that the adjacent ground was owned by Mr. Knaggs and was used by James McCarthy, Newfoundwell. He called for a Committee to be set up to consider whether it would be desirable to extend or to have a new cemetery in another part of the town. Daly again raised the question, six months later, in October 1885., and was told that the Corporation was looking at various sites in and around the town. After a lenghty discussion the matter was dropped. More lengthy meetings, during the closing years of the eighties, failed to arrive at a decision on the matter.

REAL DISPUTE.

Early in June 1892, a dispute arose over the payment for the digging of a grave in the Cord, in the process of which it had been found necessary to disinter a coffin. It seems that there was a system in operation of doing this and that it was used frequently. This practice was brought to the notice of the Corporation by the consulting sanitary officer Dr. Bradley. The Corporation, in haste, reported to the Local Government Board, who immediately ordered a public inquiry into the state of the Cord. This inquiry was held in the new Courthouse in Fair Street. It opened on 24th August 1892. It lasted four days and nearly one thousand witnesses laid claims to the graves of their dead in the Cord. An additional four hundred laid their claims with the Town Clerk, Mr. Peter Connolly.

From a summary of the inquiry furnished by the Local Government Inspector, it appeared that the Medical Officer, Dr. J.V. Byrne described the Cord as having its surface covered with monuments, apparently not having an unoccupied spot in it, and having been buried in over and over again.

The Treasurer of the Burial Committee, Mr.P.Byrne, stated that during the two years in which he had been acting in that capacity, there had been 645 interments. Other valuable information as to the condition of the cemetery was supplied by the Secretary of the Committee, Rev. John Woods. CC., Alderman R. J .Kennedy, Francis Moss, and the caretaker, Denis Kenny.

ORDER TO CLOSE THE CORD.

The minutes of the inquiry covered 860 pages, the result being the issuing by the Local Government Board, of a Sealed Order closing the Cord by 1st April 1893. Thirty-two perches known as the New Ground, at the north end of Thomas Street - an addition to this burying ground, made about 1860 - and the vaults under the Mortuary Chapel, were exempt from this order. There was widespread consternation among the townspeople, who, it may be remarked, in claiming right of burial, in many instances for seven and eight persons in the same plot, furnished unconsciously, the very evidence which closed the greater portion of the burial ground. The Corporation now had no alternative but to take immediate steps to procure a site for a new burial ground. They were placed in a dilemma. After all it was the duty of the Corporation, under the Act, to provide a burial place f or the dead.

FINAL CLOSURE

In the meantime the Corporation heard that Monsignor Robert Murphy, PP. St.Peter's, had bought a field "down the Twenties" which he was going to convert into a graveyard. The LGB, when requested, granted a stay of three months on the Cord closure, to lst July, which again, put the Corporation under pressure. Discussions took place, and the sale of the field, to Mons.`Murphy was sanctioned. The LGB granted a further stay of three months to 1st October 1893, when the Cord was finally closed.
(Most of the above, which is relevant to the Cord, has been taken <u>from-St.Peter's Parish Cemetery</u>, J.Garry. 1993.)

The Cord Cemetery

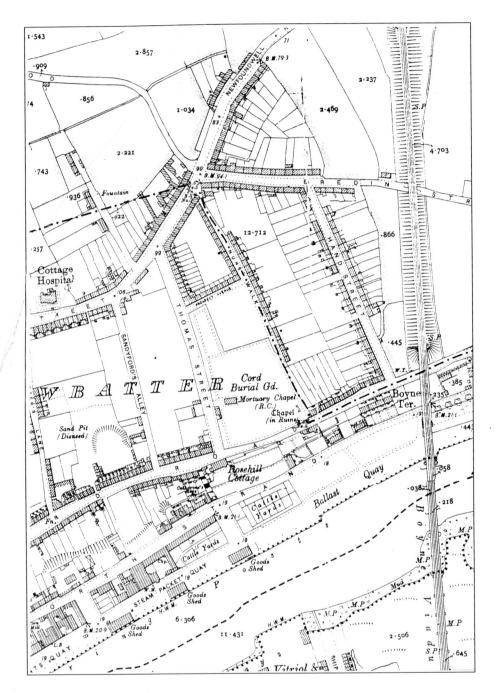

The immediate environs of the Cord Burial Ground, as seen on the 1908 map of Drogheda. Surrounded by Prospect Avenue, Nun's Walk, Cord Road and Thomas Street, in a clockwise direction.
To the south of the cemetery is Rosehill Cottage, once the home of the Grahams. It is now built upon by some twenty six houses beside Catherine's Steps (1998-99). Note that the east side of Thomas Street has no buildings and there are only two houses in Sandyford's Alley. Further north is Scarlet Street and the Cottage Hospital, built and opened in 1907. To the right is the Boyne Viaduct and the railway line behind Hand Street.

SUBSEQUENT BURIALS

Thus the graveyard was closed to burials, except for those to whom the right of interment in their family grave had been reserved. A random search of the list has, William Bannon.1919; Michael Daly, Publican, 36 Shop Street, 1965; Mary Stokes, Stockwell Lane, aunt of James E. Murphy.TD. 1944; John Dowd, 54 Laurence Street, Mayor, 1957; Michael A. Casey's first wife and children, 1896, 1907 and 1931; Frank Reynolds, ME. Bredin Street, 1960; Staff Lieut. Jack McEvoy, 1922, aged 22 years; Thomas and Maria Callan, Publican, Laurence Gate, 1942; Capt. Boylan's wife Rose, 1906; Edward Boylan, 1957; Capt. Branigan's second wife, Kate, 1929. The most recent burial, is taken from a death insertion, Mary Segrave, 9 St.Finian's Park, 1981.

BLESSING OF THE GRAVES

CEMETERY CLEAN UP

During St.Peter's Cemetery, Blessing of the Graves at the end of June 1942, the Parish Priest, Mons. O'Callaghan, made the suggestion, that if the Cord was cleaned up and made ready, he would perform a Blessing of the Graves there, in the not too distant future. The *Drogheda Independent* for 22nd August 1942 has the following:

"For the first time in many years, the Blessing of the Graves took place in the Cord Cemetery, on Sunday last 16th August. A large gathering of parishioners, was present in the old graveyard, which except for occasional burials in old family plots and vaults, has been closed for many years.

Overgrown with grass and weeds through which the hundreds of tombstones, many dating from centuries past were barely visible, the historic burial place had up to recently presented an appearance of sad neglect. Since the suggestion was made by the Rev. Archdeacon at the end of June, an amazing change has taken place. The Catholic Young Men's Society and many young men of the Parish, had worked unceasing, cutting down the grass and weeds, trimming trees and removing the accumulated debris of the passing years. Ancient monuments and headstones and the ruins of the old church are again clearly visible and provide plenty of material for students of local history. The ceremony of Blessing of the Graves was performed by Rev.Mons. O'Callaghan, assisted by Rev. T.P.Conlon, CC. Rev. P.McDonnell, CC. and Rev. M.Walsh, CC., was crossbearer. Rosary, followed with Benediction of the Blessed Sacrament. The Monsignor in thanking the C.Y.M.S. for undertaking the work of putting the Cord into decent repair, said, "anyone who visited the cemetery two months ago, and again, that day, could see the transformation that had taken place"

An 18th century view of Drogheda from the Old Jail in Scarlet Street. On the right is the present day King Street, with the town wall between two towers (Taylor's Hall and the Pigeon Tower) running down to Laurence Gate. Across the river, the wall can be seen at Curry's Hill, near James Gate, rising up to encompass the tower of the Carmelite convent in Mary's Street. To the left of this is a valley, which would be the present day Dale. The two towers beside Millmount is probably Duleek Gate, built on the same style as Laurence Gate. The town wall continues to the right of Millmount and eventually slopes down towards the river. (by permission of the County Louth Archaeological Journal. VII. 1931.)

THE LOST BURIAL REGISTER

A letter to the Editor of the Drogheda Independent. 19th September 1942 has the following:

> Dear Sir...
>
> Close on forty years ago I called on the caretaker in the Gate Lodge of the Cord Cemetery, and asked him could he locate the grave of a near and dear relative interred there 25 years earlier. He opened a large, old book, with a well worn. brown leather cover, and he soon found the name, date of burial and plot which he then pointed out. I wished I could bring the book home and read it from cover to cover. A man named Kenny was the caretaker.
>
> About 20 years ago, while trying to unravel a little antiquarian difficulty, it occurred to me to consult the Cord Cemetery Book for the solution, When I called at the Gate Lodge, I found an old woman in occupation; the former caretaker had left there, and no one seemed to know where he was. The Local Government Board had closed the Cord against burials, with some exceptions. I wonder had they also taken the Cemetery Book for safe custody? I made enquiries at the Presbytery, and from two members of the Corporation who lived on the Cord Road (and took an interest in the Cemetery) but none of them could throw any light on the subject. Has the Cord Book gone the way of many of our ancient manuscripts and ended in a blaze, but not of glory?
>
> If the Book exists, it is the property of the people of Drogheda, a large part of whose history it contains, and it should be returned to Drogheda and deposited in the Library, where it can be consulted by historians. During the cholera years, thousands of Drogheda people died of the Plague and were buried en masse in that cemetery, beyond the little chapel (and parallel to the Cord Road.)
>
> Now that the cemetery has been cleaned up, it would be opportune for antiquarians and historians to come together and appoint a number of themselves to examine every monument and headstone (erect or flat) decipher the inscriptions, take a copy of those that would throw any light on local history, and awaken an interest amongst the people in their ancestors. I am, dear sir, yours truly.
>
> "ALLENSIS"

Enquiries over the past three decades, failed to discover the whereabouts of this Register. As recently as 1995, when requested, the Secretary of the Louth County Council, the Town Clerk, Drogheda Corporation and the Parish Priest of St. Peter's, Drogheda, all confirm that they have not got the Register.

PAT CORIGAN Sculptor

A Nativity Scene is an unusual idea for the embellishment of a headstone. Four similarly executed and nearly identical versions of this have been noted, one at Dromin (Ann Hand, 1805) and three at Termonfeckin, to members of the McDonnell, King and Sheridan (1818-19-20) families respectively. McDonnell, only has "P. Corigan,Sculps.", and all stones have additional ornamentation down the sides, and

Rubbing of a Corigan Signature.

perhaps are by Corigan. Little is known of the artist, some say he had his workshop in Newtownstalaban, near Drogheda, from c1790 to 1820, and worked from a "pattern book" which showed Crucifix, Altar, Candles and Angels, Weighing of Souls, Raising of the Cross, Last Judgement, etc. Whilst most are not signed, they could be the work of Corigan. The Toner stone in the Cord, "Erected by Michael Toner of Townrath, 1792". (No.709) depicts the nativity of Our Lord, with side ornamentation, is signed near the base of the stone, by Pat Corigan. It is one of the many other examples of late Eighteenth and early Nineteenth Century decorated headstones in Co. Louth

THE INSCRIPTIONS

Fieldwork, in the terrible condition of the cemetery, with dense growth, weeds, bramble bushes, etc, started in 1971 and continued as conditions improved, with the natural seasonable cutback of the ground and weather, and this advantage was taken, as time allowed. The growth, which obscured some of the stones, was literary cut down, to expose the inscription, and was left as such, after reading and transcription. The following list, in alphabetical order, is as the stones were seen above ground. and it is not complete, as further fieldwork, will expose many tombstones which are now covered by earth, and will require a "prob search", when the cemetery is cleared of the excessive growth. and the present condition is improved. There are 957 inscriptions, as seen, up to 30th September 1977. Twenty-one stones were found to be lying face down and it was impossible to record them. A number in brackets, at the end of each inscription, corresponds with a number on a map of the graveyard. The map is not to scale and only shows approximate positions of the stones. The list also includes the wording of two plaques which originally hung in the Mortuary Chapel, and are now stored in the vaults, for safe keeping. These vaults contain fourteen coffins, in different niches, along the full length of the chapel. Because of their position, and danger of disentergration, if lifted, it was only possible to read nine plates and these are also included. Where available, further information on the deceased concerned, has been appended by the author, and this appears, in italics, underneath the inscription

THE NAME

All the O.S. Maps show 'CORD ROAD' and 'CORD BURIAL GROUND', Therefore, the word "CORD" is used throughout this study.

'CORD' derives from the long knotted cord which was worn round the waist by the friars of St. Laurence.

Example of P. Corigan's decorated stone like the 'Toner' in the Cord Cemetery.

SOURCES USED

History of Drogheda. John D'Alton. 1844. i. p116-120.

History of Drogheda. Anne Hughes. 1893. p113-121.

St.Peter's Parish Cemetery. James Garry. 1993.

The Adventures of Michael Collier, Highwayman. Drogheda Argus. no date.

Some Irish Churchyard Sculpture. Ada K.Longfield (Mrs H.G.Leask) 1974.

Co .Louth Archaeological Journal. V. 1922. V. 1923.

Journal of the Old Drogheda Society. No.3. 1978/79.

Drogheda Argus. 27/6/1874.

Drogheda Independent. 22/8/1942. 19/9/1942. 13/8/1993.

Letter from Siena Convent. 15/11/1975.

Oral Information.

Athcarne Castle on the banks of the Hurley River near Duleek, is a tower house, to which a large Tudor mansion was built by Nicholas Bathe, a wealthy Meath landowner, who also built the Wooden House, at Shop Street - Laurence Street corner in 1570. It was the home of the Gernons (buried in the vaults of the Cord Mortuary Chapel). It is now in ruins.

OCCUPATIONS ON THE CORD INSCRIPTIONS

ARCHITECT	P.J.Dodd. Peter Street. 1892.
BAKER.	William Finigan. Dublin. 1751,
BOOK-BINDER.	John O'Donegan.
BREECHES MAKER,	Andrew Brannan
BROUGE MAKER.	Patrick Healy 1784.
BUILDER.	Michael Callan. 1864.
CALLENDER MAN,	James Kelly. 1799.
CARPENTER.	Thomas Dalton. 1813.
	John Meigham. 1849
CEMETERY COMMITTEE SECRETARY.	Thomas Gulshey. 1841.
COMPANION to Catherine Daum.	Joseph Daum. 1843.
COMPANION to Joseph Daum.	Ann Daum. 1831.
COOPER in Drogheda.	Patrick Carton. 1766.
CORD-WINDER.	Patrick Doughean. 1771.
CUSTOM OFFICER.	Edward McLester. 1845.
DOCTOR.	James J.Connolly. 1920.
	Patrick W.Ekins Colpe. 1876.
DROGHEDA ARGUS,	John Hughes. 1885.
ENGINEER,	James Boland. 1849. *Belfast,Juntion Rly.*
EXCISE OFFICER.	John Keane. 1864.
GOVERNOR of DROGHEDA PRISON.	Patrick Murtagh. 1871
GROCER.	James Hickey, Laurence Street. 1863.
GUNNER	Peter J Carroll, Mary Street,
	lst Brigade, N.I. Division, R.A. 1890.
HIGH SHERIFF'.	James A Clarke. 1919.
	Alderman Thomas Connolly, 1880.
H.M. 83rd REG of FOOT.	John Carroll. 1873.
J.P.	Alderman Patrick Casey, 1880.
	Alderman Patrick Casey Connolly,1894.
LINEN MANUFACTURER.	James Owens, Fair Street, 1854.
	Henry White, 1785.
MANUFACTURER.	Patrick Woods, 1804.
MARINER.	Peter Mathews.
MASTER of the Brig	*"William"*-John Carrol, 1878.
MASON.	William Shiels,
MAYOR	John Dowd, 1957.
	John Mangan, 1901
MERCHANT.	Nicholas Barron, 1800.
	Daniel Brady, 1849.
	Robert Daly, 1836.
	James Fitzsimons, 1795
	Nicholas Flinn, 1878.
	James Lynch, 1783.
	Phllip Maginnis, 1772.
	Francis O'Ferrall, 1893

The Cord Cemetery

MERCHANT.	John Slator, 1776.
	Thomas Walsh, West Street, 1826.
M.D.	Malachi Fallon, 1896.
M.E..	Frank Reynolds, Bredin Street, 1960.
M.R.I.A. I.G.E.	Finian Henry Tallon, Laurence Street, 1908.
NUNS.	Dominican Nuns, (Siena) 1792. Translated to the Convent Cemetery, Cord Road, 27/7/1972. Sisters of Charity, Eight from 1863 to 1888 Translated to St.Peter's Cemetery, 8/8/1980.
PRIEST.	Rev.Thomas Burke.O.S.D, 1844.
	Rev.Peter Maginnis, 1818
	Rev.Jno O'Ferrall,
PRINTER and STATIONER.	Anne Hughes, 111 West Street, Publisher of *History of Drogheda.* 1892.
PUBLIC REPRESENTATIVE	Thomas McKenna. North Road. 1882
R.I.C.	Serg.James Cornym, Cord Road, 1891.
	James Hanmer, 1885.
	Conistable Meehan. 1867.
R.N.	James Cooney. Chief Officer, 1908.
	James McGough, Fair Street.
	Fleet Enigineer, 1892.
SEA CAPTAIN.	Thomas Boylan., Cord Road. 1888.
	Laurence Branigan, Boyne View, 1894.
	James Fay. 54 Scarlet Street. 1891.
	Bernard Johnson, 1880.
	Michael Kelly, 1893.
	Patrick Kelly, 1868.
	Edward Kirwan, 1917.
	Andrew Leech, 1875.
	Thomas Long, 1856.
	Thomas Long. John Street. 1881.
	John Long, 1881
	James Lyons. Newfoundwell 1876.
	Laurence Morgan. 1899.
	William Reynolds.of the Barque "*Salus*, 1882.
	Thomas Shiels. Greenhills.
	Edward Toker, 1885.

SERVANT	To the Courteneys, West Street, Anne Tierney, 1890.
	To the Clintons., Dyer Street. Anne Matthews, 1847.
	To the Dalys, Shop Street. Mary Tyrrell, 1959.
	To the Pentlands. Mrs.Carty. 1853.
SKINNER.	John Walsh. 1800.
STAFF LIEUT	Jack McEvoy. 1922
SURGEON.	Thomas Lynch 1843.
	Mr.Pentland.
TAILOR/TAYLOR	Patrick Farrell. 1796.
	Patrick Maguire
TANNER,	Joseph, Fegan. 1795.
	Simon Waliron 1860
TOBACCO SPINNER.	Bernard O' Neill. 1812. " an honest good one "
TRADER	Michael. Levins. 1846.
	Patrick Byrne, Dyer Street. 1864.
	Patrick Kelly, 1855.
	Walter Kelly, Dyer Street. 1884.
U.S.ARMY	Capt.John Cooney, 18.54.
V.S.	Thomas H.Simcocks. buried in St. .Peters
WOOLLEN DRAPER	Michael Levins, 1823.

1959. View from a boatyard at the back of Ship Street (now a timber merchants yard). The Cord Chapel and Graveyard can be seen on the right middle of the Picture.
Photo: J. Garry.

The Cord Cemetery

PLACE-NAMES ON THE CORD INSCRIPTIONS

Athcarne
Arequipa, South America
Australia

Barnattin
Barrack Street
Beamore
Beaulieu
Beleek, Co. Fermanagh
Beltichburn
Black Bull
Blackbutt Lane
Boher Glas
(later Greenbatter, its translation)
Bolton Street
Boyne Terrace
Boyne View
Bray, Co.Wicklow
Bredin Street

Calcutta
Cannstown
Carntown
Carronstown
Cartown
Castledermot, Co. Kildare
Cherrymount
Cord Road
Clanes, Co. Kildare
Colpe
Cooley Bridge
Cord Street
Crooked Street

Dale
Donore
Dowth
Dublin.Gate
Dublin Road
Dublin Road. New (1826)
Duleek
Duleek Gate
Duleek Street
Dundalk
Dyer Street

Fair Street
Francis Street
Freeschool Lane

Greenbatter
Greenhills
Greenlanes
Georges Street. Great

Hand Street
Hardmans Garden
Higginstown. Co.Kildare
Hoylake, U.S.A.

James Street.
Jewett. City, Conn. U.S.A.
Johns Gate
Johns Street

Kellys Lane
King Street

Laurence Gate
Laurence Street
Laytown
Legavoren
Levins Bridge
Linen Hall
Listoke
Livins Bridge
Liverpool
Loughboy

Magdalene Street
Malahide
Mall Mill
Manimore
Marsh
Mary Street
Mell
Ministown
Millmount Terrace
Montgomery Ala.
Mornington
Mossley Belfast

22

Mountmellick, Queens County

Newfoundwell
Newry
Newtown
Newtownstalaban
Newtown Stameen, New York.
Nicholls Bridge
North King Street, Dublin
North Road
North Strand
North Quay
Nunns Walk

Old Abbey
Old Hill

Patrick Street
Patrickswell Lane
Peter Street
Philipstown
Plattin Road
Philadelphia
Plymouth
Poomna. E.I
Prospect Avenue
Punchestown Co.Kildare

Railway Terrace
Rathmullen
Richardstown
Rope Walk
Roughgrange

Sandyford Ally
Scarlet Street
Shamrock Lodge
Sheephouse
Ship Street
Shop Street
Sligo
Stameen
Steamboat Quay
Stockwell Lane
St. Louis, U.S.A.
St. Peters Cemetery
Summerhill, Drumconrath, Co.Meath.
Sunday Gate

Templemore
Termonfeckin
Texas
The Leck, Rosnaree
Thomas Street
Trinity Street
Tuam
Twenties

West Gate
West Street
Wicklow
William Street

Yellowbatter

The Cord Cemetery

CAUSES OF DEATH ON THE CORD INSCRIPTIONS
(Specified)

CHOLERA	James Boland, Mountmellick. 1849.
CONSUMPTION	John O'Toole, Irish Legion, Franco Prussion War. 1872.
DIED AT SEA	John P. Butterly, North Quay. n.d.
DIED AT SEA	Capt. Peter Kelly. 1873.
DIED AT SEA	Owen Whitehead. 1870.
DROWNED (Buenos Aires)	Capt. William Reynolds. 1882.
DROWNED (at sea)	Patrick, James and Joseph Fay, 54 Scarlet Street, .n.d.
DROWNED (at sea)	Thomas Kelly. 1876.
DROWNED (at sea)	Mortimer M. Simington. 1900
DROWNED (River Boyne)	John Dolan. 1877.
KILLED (Dublin)	Peter Kain. 1880.
KILLED (railway)	Richard Frith. 1882.
LOST AT SEA	Capt. John Long. 1.
MURDERED	Thomas Lennod, ' ho was murdered" 1773.
SHOT (St. Mary's Bridge)	James Woods. 1868.
SHOT (California)	Capt. John Cooney, U.S. Army. 1854.

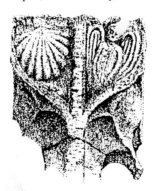

THE CORD INSCRIPTIONS

EARLIEST STONES

1613 A broken piece embedded in the ground near the ruined gable, with the lettering in relief and capital: "D THE 24 NOVEMBER 1613 AND WAS SONN. Said to be from the St. Laurernce (Howth) Tomb.

1735	Cham
1739	Roe
1741	Walsh
1749	McDonnell (Carrolan plot)
1751	Finegan
1755	Lee
1759	Chester
1760	Brackinng, Ryely
1761	Ceggly
1764	Clarke, Lyons
1766	Carton, Dardis
1768	White
1769	Cullen. Deaz. Douney
1770	Drumgoole, Plunkett
1771	Clarke, Corman, Monghean
1772	Maginnis
1773	Chester. Lennod. McKanna
1774	Cahil. Devin. Finegan. Larkin
1775	Clarke. Gorman. Monaghan
1776	Slator
1777	McKowme
1778	Deaz,. Dowdall, Lee
1781	Clark, Gibbons,. Hardman. Kell Winne
1782	Cullen, Lynch
1784	Healy, McGough, Newgent
1788	Murtagh. Patterson
1790	Fitzsimions
1790	Divin
1796	Farrell
1799	Deven., Kelly, McQuail

James Garry October 1988.

The Cord Cemetery

VAULTS IN THE CORD MORTUARY CHURCH,

On 15th September 1973 Mr. Brendan Walker and Miss Deirdre Crilly, of the Drogheda branch of the Red Cross, helped Jim Garry of the Old Drogheda Society, to move down to the vaults - for safe keeping - a marble plaque. Which had been thrown out of the church. during alterations of the building to suit Red Cross purposes. The Plaque has the following inscription:

> "Of' your charity pray for the soul of.
> MARY McDONOUGH, relict of the late MATHEW McDONOUGH of
> Drogheda who died 6th Feb.1877 aged 83 years.
> LOUISE wife of EDWARD McDONOUGH who died
> 5th March, 1908 and of EDWARD McDONOUGH.who died
> 19th February 1917. May they rest in peace.

Another small plaque was also taken down and placed beside the coffin bearing the name and date - THOMAS SHUEMAN 1st Feb.1875. This plaque just had the legend :

"Erected by Mrs Kate Shueman in memory of her dearly beloved husband Thomas Shueman who departed this life lst Feb1875"

In the Vaults there are fourteen coffins in different niches along the full length of the church. Because of their position and danger of disintergration, if moved, it was only possible to read nine (9) plates. They are as follows:

DUFFY:	Jane wife of John Duffy, died 23rd Jan, 1903.
GERNON:	Alice Louise Gernon, 4th Dec, 1916.
GERNON:	Margaret Gernon, 13th Feb.1891, aged 84.
KEAPPOCK:	James Keappock, 2nd March 1898.
MAGILL:	Henry Magill, 30th Dec1899, aged 80 years.
MAGILL:	Mrs. Catherine Magill, 13th March 1900, aged 87 years.
McDONOUGH:	Edward McDonough, l9th Feb.1917.
McDONOUGH:	Louise McDonough, 5th March 1908.
SHUEMAN':	Thomas Shueman, lst Feb 1875

- McDonoughs were at 113 West Street just before James Magee started business there in 1906.

- James Keappock.was a hotel owner where the White Horse Hotel now is in West Street.

- The Gernons were in Athcarne Castle (just outside Duleek) up to about forty years ago. It is now in ruins.

The vaults are clean and dry and kept under lock. The key is with the caretaker (Mr. Dermot Hoey) in the nearby Cord Lodge. A gargoyle base which stood at the corner of the church was also put in the vaults on this date. Two pictures of this may be seen in CLAJ. XI 1945.

James Garry 1st September 1974

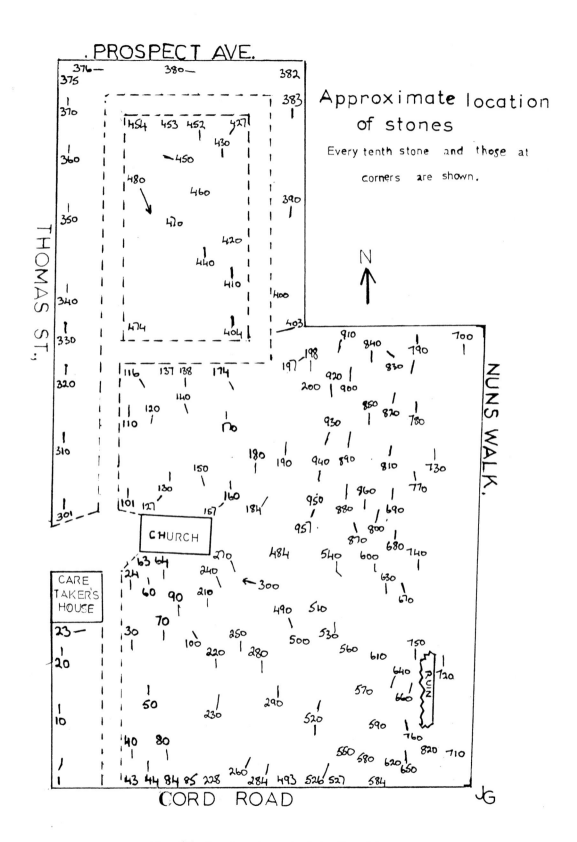

Map of the Cemetery. Approximate location of stones.

ALLEN
Erected by Thomas Allen of Laytown to the memory of his wife Mary who died 9th April 1880 aged 25 years.

(183)

ANDERSON
Erected by the Rev. James A. Anderson, O.S.A. to the memory of his father John Anderson who died in the 31st year of his age, 1840. Of his brother William Anderson who died 10th March 1864 aged 27 years. Also his cousins Eliza O'Toole who died 24th September 1867 aged 19 years and John O'Toole who died of consumption contracted while serving in the Irish Legion during the late Franco Prussian War, 19th July 1872 aged 27 years.

(197)

(Fr. Anderson was born in Drogheda "in the shadow of Laurence Gate" in 1837
and died in Dublin in 1903. Always a controversial figure, his name was to become synonomous with many contentious issues in the latter part of the 19th century. He was Prior of the "Low Lane" church in 1879. Always a man of action in a short time he was organising a pilgrimage from Drogheda to the new shrine of Our Lady at Knock. It is believed that this was the first ever organised pilgrimage to Knock. See JODS No.11. 1998. p 145-152 for account of the pilgrimage by Iggy O'Donovan. OSA. Fr.Anderson's mother Alice (nee Kelly) is buried in Tullyallen.)

Fr. James A. Anderson O.S.A

ANDREWS
This stone was erected by John Andrews in memory of his beloved wife
Margaret who departed this life 13th August 1832 aged 21 years. Also her mother who died 10th June 1832 aged 60.

(880)

ARNOLD
Erected by Edward Arnold in memory of his father Edward who departed this life 18th April 1836 aged 84 years.

(929)

ASPIL
Erected by Nicholas Aspil, Bolton Street, in loving memory of his wife Anne who died 6th February 1874 aged 58 years. Also his daughter Charlotte aged 15 years. Also the above Nicholas who died June 10th 1885, aged 72 years.

(149)

AUSTIN
See Brown.

(634)

BAGNALL
Erected 1st January 1842 by John Bagnall for him and his posterity and also his son Bernard who died in the 3rd year of his age. Here also is interred the said John Bagnall who died on the 30th September 1846 aged 49 years.

(496)

BAGNAL
Erected by John Bagnal, Peter Street, in memory of his sister Jane who died 21st December 1867, his mother Charlotte who died February 1802. His brother George, 15th August 1884 and his father George died December 1888.

(497)

BAGNAL
Erected by William Bagnal of Drogheda in memory of his wife Mary who departed 30th April 1857 aged 75 years. Also his son George aged 26 years and Robert aged 23 years. Also the above William Bagnall, died 13th February 1858 aged 78 years.

(818)

BANKS
See Kelly.

(801)

BANNION
Erected by John Bannion in memory of his father and two of his children who died young.

(297)

BANNON
Have mercy O'Lord on the souls of Teresa, wife of William Bannon, West Street, Drogheda, who died 8th March 1884 and Teresa Angela daughter of the above who died 1st April 1891 aged 8 years and the above William who died 23rd July 1919. Sarah A. Connolly daughter of the above died 16th September 1941.

(370)

BARKER
Erected by William Barker in memory of his children Mary Ellen and William Joseph who died 31st December 1872. Also his son Thomas Joseph died 1st December 1889 aged 21 years. Also his wife Rose Ann died 19th January 1889, the above William Barker died 16th June 1892 and his daughter Rosa who died 26th May 1898 aged 13 years.

Also his sisters Sarah died 10th October 1898 and Hannah died 1st January 1905, his son John Joseph died 20th June 1909 and his brother Robert J. who died in New York 7th December 1913.

(379)

(When William Barker died, his family presented the Mass Bell, to the new St. Mary's Church in James Street, "to his memory". My grandmother, Margaret Nulty (nee Watters), 7 Marsh Road, (d.1964), always referred to the sound, at the Angelus, as "Barker's Bell". She remembered as a child, playing in and around the bell as it lay in James Street, before it was hung in the Bell Tower of the church. According to Fred E. Dukes in his "Bells of Drogheda", the bell weighs 30 cwt, and was cast in 1893 by Byrne of Dublin. It was consecrated on 20th May 1894. The inscription is in Latin."St. Mary Church, Drogheda. The Gift of William Barker. John Curry, Pastor."William Barker was described as a widely respected business man in James Street.)

BARRETT
Erected by Andrew Barrett of Drogheda in memory of his son Patrick Barrett who died 14th May 1804 aged 16 years also four more of his children who died young. His father John Barrett died 9th May 1805 aged 76 years. And the above Andrew Barrett died 17th June 1805 aged 37 years.
(578)

BARRON
Erected to the memory of Anne Barron late of Old Hill, Drogheda, who died 18th August 1842 aged 63 years.
(663)

BARRON
Erected AD.1800 by Nicholas Barron of Drogheda, Merchant.
(767)

BATH
See Duffy.
(684)

BEAHAN
In memory of Owen Beahan of Duleek who departed this life 11th May 1866 and his infant daughter Catherine who died 12th May 1863.
(899)

BEAHAN
This Stone and Burial Place erected by Owen Beahan of Punchestown, County Kildare, and now of Drogheda, for him and his posterity and in memory of his wife Anne who lieth beneath and died the 15th January 1828 aged 45 years. Also his eldest daughter Margaret who died 9th April 1852 aged 40 years.
(900)

BEGBEY
Erected by John Begbey of Drogheda in memory of his father William Begbey who died 3rd Sept. 1822 aged 42 years. Also his brother William who died an infant.
(551)

BELTON
Erected by Thomas Belton in memory of his father Patk. Belton died July 4th 1837 aged 47 years, late out Laurence Gate. And also his mother Mary Belton who died 13th May 1854 aged 56 years. His brother Patrick Belton, 24th August 1858 aged 25 years. And the above Thomas Belton died 6th February 1867.
(590)

BELL
Erected by Rose Bell in memory of her husband Christopher Bell who died 29th January 1838 aged 51 years and her son Thomas Bell who died 16th July 1832 aged 14 years.
(826)

BELLEW
Erected by Mr. James Bellew of North Quay Drogheda in memory of his daughter Mary Anne who died 15th of May 1850 aged 21. Pray for the soul of poor Mary Anne. And the above James Bellew died the 11th January 1876 aged 65 years.

(940)

BERRILL
Erected to the memory of Thomas Berrill of Hand Street who died 17th July 1879 and his wife Jane who died 16th October 1883. Also their daughters Maria and Monica who died 10th October 1874 and 10th August 1875 respectively.

(314)

BERRILL
Erected by John Berrill in memory of his mother Margaret Berrill, King St. Drogheda, who died 2nd June 1851 aged 41 years and his father Patrick Berrill who died 6th March 1866 aged 69 years.

(507)

BERRILL
Erected by Mary Berrill in memory of her husband Peter Berrill of Laurence Gate who died 4th October 1873.

(732)

BERRILL
Sacred to the memory of Catherine the beloved wife of Barth'w Berrill of Drogheda. She departed this life 10th September 1830 in the 30th year of her age. Also interred are the remains of two of their infant children.

(736)

BIGGERS
Erected by Mrs. Alicia Biggers of West Street, Drogheda, in memory of her husband Matthew Biggers who died October 4th 1866. Of your charity pray for the repose of the souls of the above - Alicia Biggers died 26th February 1880 and her son James who died 26th May 1892 aged 43 years and her daughter Margaret who died December 15th 1893.

(52)

BIRD
Erected by Eliza Bird in memory of her husband Michael Bird who died 4th May 1872 aged 60 years and her son Nicholas who died 15th October 1876 aged 19 years.

(198)

BIRON
Here lyeth the body of Eliza Biron who departed this life 10th May 1814 aged twenty-four years.

(933)

BISSET
See Kirwan.

(528)

BISSETT
Erected to the memory of James Bissett. May he rest in peace.

(946)

BLACK
Erected by Michael Black, Colpe, in memory of his wife Catherine who died Sep 2nd 1890 aged 50 years and her son James died May 27th 1913 aged 43 years, also the above Michael Black who died 5th February 1917 aged 90 years.

(383)

BLAKE
See also his mother Margaret died 7th February 1876 aged 60 years.

(876)

BOGAN
See Gamble.

(737)

BOLAND
Erected by James Boland Esq, Mountmellick, Queens Co, in memory of his beloved and virtuous son Thomas who died 5th of August 1849 at the residence of E. Moore, Esq., Shamrock Lodge. He died of Cholera caught in the faithful discharge of his duties as Engineer of the Belfast Junction Railway in his 22nd year, having accomplished the virtues of mature age and resigned his soul unto the hands of Him who gave it. He exchanged his prospects in this vale of tears for a better portion in the Society of the Just.

(331)

BOWEN
Erected by Mary Bowen in memory of her husband William Bowen who died 11th July 1877 and her father James Fitzsimons who died 10th September 1867.

(790)

BOYLAN
Erected by Captain Thomas Boylan of Cord Road, Drogheda, Born 1807. In memory of his three children Nicholas, Bartle and Thomas who died young. The above Captain Thomas Boylan died 9th January 1888 aged 81 years. Also his wife Rose Boylan died 6th October 1906.

(112)

BOYLAN
Erected by Edward Boylan of Yellowbatter, in memory of his son Edward who departed this life 2nd May 1881 aged 8 years. Also the above Edward Boylan who died 2nd February 1887 aged 69 years. His son William died 5th February 1894 and his wife Elizabeth who died 14th June 1904 aged 71 years. His son James died 29th October 1925 aged 65 years and his wife Mary Jane died 26th September 1936 also Annie Skelly daughter of Edward Boylan died 10th January 1957 aged 88 years.

(479)

BOYLAN
Erected by Elizabeth Boylan of James St, in memory of her mother Anne Boylan who died 2nd December 1879 aged 61 yrs.

(565)

BOYLAN
Erected by James Boylan of Patrick Street, Drogheda in memory of his wife Mary who died 26th May 1843, aged 60 years.

(871)

BOYLAN
See Sisters of Charity.

(1)

BOYLAN
See Byrne.

(835)

BOYLE
Erected by Mrs. Boyle, Boyne Terrace, in memory of Mr. Daniel Boyle late of Dundalk who died 7th of February 1859.

(108)

BOYLE
See Kelly.

(523)

BOYLE
See Byrne.

(953)

BRACKINNG
This Stone and Burial Place belongeth to James Brackinng. Here lieth three of his children 1760.

(278)

BRADLEY
Margaret Bradley erected this stone in memory of her husband Edward Bradley who died 10th June 1839 aged 49 years and his son Patrick died 23rd August 1870.

(669)

BRADY
Erected by Andrew Brady in memory of his mother Anne Brady died 16th May 1854. His father Patk Brady died 28th April 1864 and his son Patk died 23rd March 1866 aged 5 years.

(119)

BRADY
Erected by Bernard Brady of Dyer Street, in memory of his children. Ellen died 25th Jan 1882 aged 17 years. Mary Anne died 6th March 1882 aged 18 years and Patrick and Eliza who also died young. The above Bernard who died 22nd May 1884 aged 57 years and his wife Mary died 1st November 1893 aged 50 years.

(250)

BRADY
To the memory of Honora Brady.

(836)

BRADY
Erected by Mr. Daniel Brady of Drogheda, Merchant, in memory of his son Daniel who died 20th February 1839 in the eighth year of his age. Also his daughter Eliza who died 11th May 1847 in the eighteenth year of her age. The above Daniel Brady died 19th of September 1849 aged 52 years. Deeply and deservedly regretted he passed away from this life accompanied by the prayers and good wishes of all who knew him for his eternal welfare in another and happier world, also his son Thomas C. Brady who died 19th June 1882 aged 51 years.
(939)

BRADY
See Devin insertion

BRANAGAN
See Byrne.
(953)

BRANIGAN
Erected by Captain Laurence Branigan of Boyne View, Drogheda, to the memory of his beloved wife Mary who departed this life 30th day of July 1873 and her two children who died young. Also his daughter Mrs. Margaret Fay who died 13th April 1880.
Also the above Capt. Laurence Branigan who died on 21st October 1894 and his second wife Kate who died 7th February 1929.
(330)

BRANIGAN
In loving memory of Mrs. Mary Branigan who died 26th December 1865 aged 77 years.
(63)

BRANGAN
In memory of Thomas Brangan of Ministown who died 18th July 1885 aged 75 years. His wife Mary died 16th March 1890 aged 55 years. Their son John who died 8th April 1912, their daughter Agnes died 24th April 1913 and two sons James died 8th August 1930 and Patrick died 16th August 1941 and their daughters Margaret died 27th January 1938, Mary died 4th November 1942 and Kate died 30th November 1944.
(377)

BRANNAN
This Buriel Place belongeth to Andrew Brannan, Breeches Maker of Drogheda.
Here lieth five of his family.
(577)

BRAY
John Bray died 18th July 1868 aged 41 years. Erected by his son Michael. Also his son Patrick died 10th July 1865 aged 4 years.
(537)

BRENNAN
Of your charity pray for the souls of Patrick Brennan who died 19th July 1878, of his wife Judith who died 8th July 1852 and of his father Patrick Brennan and his brother James.
(204)

BRENNAN
See Gibbons.
(245)

BRENNAN
See Tiernan.
(595)

BRIEN
Erected by Anne Brien of Duleek Street, in memory of her father and mother Peter and Mary Brien and her brother Peter who died 21st May 1882.
(793)

BRIODY
In memory of Charles and Rose Briody of Mary Street who died - the former 25th August 1885 and the latter 28th June 1387, also their children Daniel, Margaret and Anne who are interred here.
(440)

BRODIE
1866 Erected by Mrs. Brodie of John St, in memory of her mother Anne Caffrey and her brother John Caffrey whose remains are interred here.
(116)

BRODIGAN
Erected by Peter Brodigan in memory of his father and mother Patrick and Anne Brodigan who died 1863 and 1866.
(682)

BROGAN
To the memory of Richard Brogan, Platten Road, died 17th August 1898 aged 75 years. Also his son-in-law Patrick Farrell died 31st January 1897 aged 48 years and his son Thomas died 31st January 1905 aged 34 years. His son Richard died 14th August 1910 aged 46 years. Also Elizabeth wife of the above Richard Junior, who died 17th July 1916 aged 45 years.
(439)

BROOKS
Erected by Francis Brooks of Old Hill, in memory of his beloved Catherine who died 12th September 1882 aged 60 years.
(87)

BROWN
Erected by Sarah Brown to the memory of her husband Andrew Brown of Sunday Gate, Drogheda, who died 13th November 1812 aged 52 years. Here likewise are interred the remains of the above-named Sarah Brown who died 3rd March 1814 in the 39th year of her age. Also her daughter Mary Austin who died 29th February 1816 aged 42. Also her great-grand-daughter Elizabeth Austin who

died 1821 aged 2 years. Her grandson Robert Austin who died 31st July 1828 aged 24 years. Her grand-daughter Mary Anne Tierney who died 15th January 1863 aged 76 years.

(634)

BROWN
See Read.

(633)

BURKE
This Monument has been erected in memory of the late Rev. Thomas Burke, O.S.D. A man deservedly respected for his sincere piety and admired for Zeal in promoting the Cause of Temperance among the inhabitants of Drogheda. He died on 29th of October 1844. May he rest in peace.

(754)

Monument of Rev. Thomas Burke, O.S.D., beside the ruined gable.

(Fr.Thomas Burke of the Linen Hall chapel, launched a Harp Society in 1839, and was also President of the Drogheda Total Abstinence Society founded in 1840. Although Burke played the harp himself, he brought a teacher from Belfast. A German tourist, Johann Kohl visited Drogheda in 1843 and was impressed, when the Society gave a public performance, organised as a "musical poetical soiree".
Fr.Burke's name is on the Temperance Banner in Millmount Museum.

BURKE
Erected by Michael Burke, Cord Road, in memory of his children: Stephen James died 27th Dec 1872 aged 5½ years, Dominick Francis and Bridget Teresa who all died young. And Mary Anne who died 18th February 1890 aged 22 years.

(863)

BURKE
In memory of the children of Francis Burke.
James died April 1877 aged 15 years.
Patrick died August. 1891 aged 15 years,
Also Teresa Ellen and Frank who died young.

(28)

BUTTERLY
Erected by Peter Butterly of North Quay, Drogheda, in memory of his mother Anne Butterly who died December 1878 aged 68 years. His father John Butterly who died January 1847 aged 47 years. iHis brother John Patrick Butterly who died at sea aged 20 years. Here also are interred his grand-father and grand-mother George and Jane Butterly and his sister Rose Butterly who died 19th October 1882.

(511)

BUTTERLY
Erected in memory of Mr. John Butterly formerly of North Quay and late of Barrack Street, Drogheda, who died 26th March 1893 aged 85 years.

(653)

BUTTERLY
See Woodlock.

BUTTERLY
See Farrell.

Thomas Butterly Contractor Builder of the Cord Mortuary Chapel. Courtesy Marie Carolan.

(661)

(850)

BURNS
Erected by Robert Burns of Trinity Street, in memory of his wife Mary Burns who died 1st November 1874 aged 48 years. Also the above named Robert Burns died 6th September 1885.

(789)

BURNS
See Heeney.

(930)

BYRNE
Erected by Bernard Byrne of Dyer Street, in memory of his wife Margaret who died 2nd March 1877 aged 60 years and two of their children, Mary and Eliza who died young. The above Bernard died 20th September 1880 and his son Patrick who died 15th July 1886.

(163)

BYRNE
Erected by Mary Byrne in memory of her sister Margaret Farrell.

(199)

BYRNE
Erected by Patrick Byrne of Great Georges Street, Drogheda, in memory of his brother Thomas died 22nd May 1842 aged 44 years. His daughters Elizabeth died 6th July 1838 aged 18 years and Bridget 5th January 1840 aged 16 years.

(222)

BYRNE
Erected by Thomas Byrne of Drogheda, in memory of his daughter Elizabeth who died 21st May 1832 aged 23 years.

(271)

BYRNE
Erected by Francis Byrne, Hardmans Garden, in memory of his mother Margaret Byrne died 18th April 1885. Also his brothers John and Thomas.

(281)

BYRNE
To the memory of Andrew Byrne who died 30th September 1867 aged 31 years.

(405)

BYRNE
Erected by Patrick Byrne, Bredin St, in memory of his wife Anne who died 25th March 1804 and their sons Francis who died 7th August 1881 and Joseph - who died at Santos 1891. Also their grandson Patrick J. Dowd and the above Patrick who died 15th November 1905. Also their daughters Mary Anne

Connor died 22nd December 1926 and Margaret Dowd died 22nd October 1935 and her daughter Mary who died 24th October 1958.

(406)

BYRNE
Erected by Matthew Byrne, Newtown, Drogheda, in memory of his father Patrick died 2nd Sept 1884 also his brother John died 7th January 1888.

(449)

BYRNE
Erected by Martin Byrne, Greenhills, in memory of his mother-in-law Jane Cooney who died 1st December 1858 aged 63 years and his daughter Jane who died 6th March 1859 aged 18 years.

(501)

BYRNE
To the memory of Charles Byrne of Drogheda and his wife Bridget who died 6th June 1879.

(543)

BYRNE
Erected by Michael Byrne of Sundays Gate, in memory of his son Thomas who died 18th April 1851 aged 14 months and his cousin James Kearns who lies underneath.

(766)

BYRNE
Erected by Michael Byrne of Drogheda, in memory of his brother John Byrne who departed this life the 10th February 1831 aged 37 years.

(778)

BYRNE
Erected by Terence Byrne, Scarlet St, in memory of Patrick Boylan who departed this life 2nd March 1856 aged 25 years. Also his father and mother Patrick and Margaret Boylan
Also John and Alice Lynes father and mother-in-law to the above Terence Byrne.
Also Francis Torron nephew to the above Patrick Boylan who died 2nd July 1875 aged 28 years. Also James Lynes brother-in-law to the above Terence Byrne died 9th January 1883.

(835)

BYRNE
Erected by Alice Byrne in memory of her mother Mary Byrne late of 70 West Street, died 19th July 1888. Also her sister Mary Richards died 10th March 1891.

(869)

BYRNE
Erected by Mr Patrick Byrne of West St. to the memory of his uncle Mr. Patrick Byrne late of West St. who died July 21st 1849 aged 68 years. Also Mary Byrne died 17th January 1852.
Also Anne Margaret the beloved child of Patrick Byrne who died 17th January aged 11 months.

(952)

BYRNE
As a tribute of affectionate respect. This tomb was placed here to the memory of Mr Charles Byrne late of Dyer Street by his widow Margaret. He died 17th June 1817. Underneath lie the remains of their son James. He died 17th April 1832 and William son of Mr Owen Boyle of West Street and nephew of the above who died 27th August 1832. The above Margaret Byrne died 7th April 1958. And Patrick Byrne T.C Dyer St. son of Charles died 25th June 1864. Also Judith Branagan who died 15th October 1875 daughter of the above. Charles and Margaret Branagan died 22nd November 1876.

(953)

BYRNE
See Maginn.

(274)

BYRNE
See Magee.

(286)

DEATH OF PROMINENT SEAMAN
We regret to record the death of Captain James Butler, which took place at his residence, Wellington Place, on Monday last. Captain Butler, who , though enjoying until some months ago the most robust health, had reached a ripe old age, and had been for many years in command of the one the Dundalk and Newry Steam Packet Company's vessels. "The Emerald Isle" and in that capacity won the esteem of all with whom he came in contact. The funeral took place on Wednesday at the Cord Cemetery, Drogheda, and was largely attended. The pall bearers were Messers T. Brown, R.L Brown, J.P. Thomas Connick, J.D.O'Neill, R.H. Doherty Town Clerk of Newry, and S. Kelly. The chief mourners were - Mr John Burns and Mr Martin, Drogheda. The funeral services was recited by Rev. J. Smyth. C.C. and Rev P Fagan, C.C Dundalk.

'Dundalk Democrat' Saturday 9th June 1888

CAFFREY
Erected by Michael Caffrey of Trinity St., in memory of his wife and relatives.

(118)

CAFFREY
Erected by Patrick Caffrey of Drogheda, in memory of his son Joseph who died 5th March 1835 aged 22 years. Also his son James died 17th January 1841 aged 22 years. His wife Catherine died 11th July 1849 aged 65 years and the above Patrick Caffrey who died 15th March 1850 aged 74 years. Here also is interred his daughter Mary who died 16th May 1873 aged 64 years and his son Philip who died 13th September 1879 aged 68 years.

(165)

CAFFREY
Sacred to the memory of Anthony Caffrey, Scarlet Street, who died 5th April 1892 aged 72 years, and his daughter Kate who died 8th January 1874

(313)

CAFFREY
See Brodie.

(116)

CAFFREY
See Meehan.

(495)

CAHAN
This stone and Burial Place belongeth to John Cahan where lyeth six of his family 1735.

(718)

CAHIL
This Stone and Burial Place belongeth to Edward Cahil and his Posterity wherein lieth 8 of his Ancestors. Also 5 of his children 1774.

(644)

CAHILL
See Toker

(809)

CAIN
Erected by Christopher Cain in memory of his mother Alice Cain who died 25th October 1864 aged 85 years.

(21)

CALLAN
Erected by Michael Callan of Drogheda, Builder, in memory of his beloved daughter Mary Ann who died 8th August 1848 in the 20th year of her age. Also his wife Mary who died 21st January 1854 and his daughter Alitic who died 8th April 1858. The above Michael Callan who died 25th July 1864.

(35)

CALLEN
Erected by James Callan of Drogheda, in memory of his wife Jane Callan who died 14th January 1852 aged 56 years. Also his daughter Margaret who died 19th June 1848 aged 30 years and his son James died 20th November 1844 aged 9th years.

(169)

CALLAN
Erected by Thomas Callan, Laurence Gate, in memory of his children Michael Henry died 12th June 1895, Patrick Francis – 12th February 1906, the above Thomas Callan 10th March 1942 also Maria wife of the above Thomas who died 25 October 1942.

(382)

CALLAN
Erected by Michael Callan, Sunday Gate, in memory of his father Thomas Callan. Who departed this life 9th October 1850 aged 63 years. Also his mother Margaret who died 12th April 1833 aged 42 years, and his brothers who died young. Also the above Michael Callan died 17th October 1856 aged 51 years and his son Thomas who died young

(882)

CALLAGHAN
Erected by John Callaghan of Shop Street, in memory of his daughter Bridget who died November 12th 1878 and his father-in-law, John Tandy who died 20th December 1881.

(14)

CALLAGHAN
See Kirwan.

(350)

CAMPBELL
Ad 1867. Erected by Catherine Campbell, Shop Street, Drogheda, in memory of her beloved husband Owen Campbell who departed this life 19th March 1866 aged 56 years. Also their Grandchildren, Theresa Ellen Mooney who died 30th January 1875 aged 2 weeks, Lizzie who died 11th September 1876 aged 6 years & 3 months and William Alphonsus who died 18th October 1876 aged 6 months.

(7)

CAMPBELL
Anne Campbell of Scarlet Street in memory of her husband Patrick who died 12th February 1888 aged 64 years. Their son Patt. who died young.

(268)

CAMPBELL
In memory of Mrs Catherine Campbell who died December 1885 aged 78 years and her daughter Mrs Margaret Corrigan who died 5th May 1919 aged 78 years. And her son-in-law Patrick Corrigan who died 12th December 1919 aged 84 years.

(391)

CAMPBELL
In memory of Jenette Campbell, Scarlet St., who died 31st November 1921 aged 79 years. Her daughter Annie died 15th March 1954.

(395)

CAMPBELL
Erected by Christopher Campbell of Hand St. in memory of his father and mother Philip and Catherine Campbell and four of their children, Mary James, Catherine and John.

(529)

CAMPBELL
Underneath lie the remains of Eliza daughter of Mr Charles Campbell of Drogheda, who died 20th November 1818 aged six months. Also the remains of his father Mr John Campbell who died 17th March 1820 aged 71 years. Also Mrs Catherine Campbell daughter of the above Charles who died 22nd January 1837.

(668)

CAMPBELL
Erected by Patrick Campbell of Sunday's Gate, in memory of his father Thomas Campbell who died 15 Nov 1864 aged 68 years. His Uncle Patrick died 14th September 1859 aged 75 and his brother Joseph died 12th June 1867 age 22 years.

(751)

CANAVAN
Erected by Sarah Canavan in memory of her husband Charles who died on Thursday 12th April 1849 aged 47 years.

(48)

CANE
Erected by Cecelia Cane in memory of her husband Michael who died 8th May 1865 aged 64 years. The above Cecila Cane died 13th April 1869 aged 70 years.

(484)

CARR
Erected by William Carr of Hand St, in memory of his son John who died 14th January 1880 aged 3 years and 6 months. Also his wife Bridget who died the 21st March 1888.

(147)

CARR
Erected by Mary Carr in memory of her husband Patrick Carr who departed this life on the 14th November 1873 aged 76 years.

(400)

CARR
Pray for the soul of Mary Carr who died 12th December 1878 and her husband James Carr died 6th March 1882.

(515)

CARR
See McGlade.

(150)

CARR
See McCabe.

(194)

CARR
See Keappock.

(753)

CARRAHER
Erected by Laurence Carraher in memory of his son James who died the 21st May 1821 aged 22 years. Also four of his children who died young

(958)

CARROLL
Erected by James Carroll of Mornington in memory of his son Thomas who departed this life 22nd April 1866 aged 21 years. Also the above-named James Carroll who died 4th May 1869 aged 70 years and his son Peter who died the 7th April 1873 aged 24 years. Also his son John who died 22nd May 1891 aged 39 years.

(4)

CARROLL
Erected by Michael Carroll of Mornington, in memory of his beloved wife Margaret who died 16th August 1833 and four of their children who died young. Also his grandchild Mary C. Carroll and his

son John who died 26th March 1890 aged 43 years. The above named Michael Carroll who died 22nd May 1890 aged 86 years.

(5)

CARROLL

Erected by Christopher Carroll of Mell, in memory of his wife Mary who died 18th June 1879 aged 41 years and three of their children who died young

(59)

CARROLL

Erected by Mary Carroll, Mary Street, in memory of her son Peter J. Carroll who died at Plymouth, 14th September 1890 aged 24 years and was interred there, Late Gunner of No.98 1st Brigade Division R.A. Also her son Patrick who died young.

(81)

CARROLL

Erected by Thomas Carroll of James Street, in memory of his daughter Kate M. Carroll died 20th March 1886 aged 23 years.

(214)

CARROLL

Erected by Mary Carroll, Nunns Walk, in memory of her father Peter Carroll who died 7th April 1881.

(258)

CARROLL

Erected by James Carroll of Beaulieu, in memory of Catherine who died 15th September 1839 and his father Laurence who died 23rd November 1866.

(270)

CARROLL

John Carroll, Master of the Brig William of Drogheda, erected this stone in memory of his wife Rose Ann Carroll who died 16th June 1851. Also his infant sons John and Peter who died young, and of his brother Charles Carroll who died 15th January 1878 aged 48 years.

(335)

CARROLL

Erected by Peter Swithin Carroll in memory of his father John Carroll who died 27th March 1873 aged 70 years. His mother Anne Carroll who died 18th February 1872 aged 64 and his brother John Carroll died at Poona E.I., 26th January 1873, aged 22 years, late of H.M. 83rd Reg. of Foot.

(522)

CARROLL

Erected 1798 by Patrick Carroll for him and his posterity.

(553)

CARROLL

Erected by Mathew Carroll of Trinity St. His father Michael Carroll died 10th September 1850 and his mother Mary died 8th November 1865 and his sister Mary who died young.

(670)

CARROLL
See Sisters of Charity.
(1)

CARROLL
See Terney.
(60)

CARROLL
See Greene.
(371)

CARROLL
................................and of the above Mr Peter Carroll who died 29th July 1849 aged 29 years, deeply regretted by all those who knew him.
(The first part of this inscription is now illegible).
(33)

CARNEY
Glory be to God on High. Erected by John Carney of Boyne View in memory of his mother-in-law, Catherine O'Reilley late of Higginstown, Co. Longford, who died 26th January 1844 aged 90 years, and of Mary, relict of the above John Carney died 26th October 1869 aged 44 years. Also of Stephen Carney who died at Richardstown, Clane, Co. Kildare aged 44 years. It is a holy and wholesome thought to pray for the dead that they may be loosed from their sins ñ 12c Macabees 46 V.
(160)

CARNEY
In memory of Francis Woodhouse Carney beloved child of Henry and Alice Carney died 14th August 1873 aged 7 years and 8 months.
Also James Thomas Horan died 21st December 1870 aged 29 years.
(472)

CARNEY
Erected by Patrick Carney, Fair St., Drogheda, in memory of his son Michael who died 3rd July 1868 aged 15 years. Also his infant daughter Catherine who died 1st October 1869.
(702)

CAROLAN
Erected by Mrs Carolan, Mell, in memory of her brother John Reilly who died 27th December 1871. Also her mother Mrs Mary Reilly
(547)

CARROLAN
Here lyeth the body of Bridget Carrolan who resided at Duleek Gate. She was a truly upright Christian and departed this life on the 25th April 1805 aged 52 years.
(603)

CARROLAN
This Burial Place belongeth to James Carrolan. Here lyeth the body of Cullím McDonnell who died ye 7th day of September 1749 aged 60 years.

(710)

CARTEN
Erected by James Carten in memory of his father William Carten

(124)

CARTER
Erected by Mrs Rosa Carter, West St., Drogheda, in memory of her husband Patrick Carter who died 24th December 1820 aged 42 years. Also her son John who died 21st September 1843 aged 36 years, and the above Rose Carter who died 19th July 1845 aged 45 years.

(311)

CARTER
Erected by Mrs Anne Carter of Crooked Street, in memory of her husband John Carter who died 26th September 1851 aged 36 years. Also her daughter Maryanne who died young.

(600)

CARTON
This Stone and Burial Place belongeth to Patrick Carton, Cooper in Droughída and his family. Underneath lyeth fore of his children. Erected 17th May 1766

(593)

CARTY
See Pentland.

(29)

CASEY
In memory of Patrick Casey, Scarlet St., Drogheda who died June 9th 1886. Also his wife Mary who died 15th September 1888. Their son John who died 11th October 1888 and two of their children who died young also their son Thomas who died 7th May 1893 and their son Patrick who died August 4th 1893

(137)

CASEY
Pray for the soul of Ellen Mary, wife of Michael A Casey. Born at Templemore 2nd September 1863 died at Drogheda 16th August 1896 and their child Margaret Mary who died 21st September 1907 aged 14 years.

On the Reverse Side
Also their eldest child Mary Casey (Edem) who died 7th March 1931 aged 43 years.

(480)

(Michael A.Casey, a north Tipperery man was Editor of the Drogheda Independent for 50 years. He was appointed on the recommendation of Parnell and Michael Davitt. Living, first at No.2 St. Mary's Terrace, Dublin Road, he played a prominent role in the rapid development of the paper, and was succeeded by his two sons, Joachim (1939) and Peter (1940). Michael Casey and his 2nd wife are buried in St. Peter's.)

The Cord Cemetery

Michael A. Casey, Editor of the Drogheda Independent, for 50 years.

CASEY
Erected by Owen Casey, Greenbatter, Drogheda in memory of his mother Mary Casey who died 30th December 1855 aged 70 years. Also his daughter Ann who died 9th February 1873 aged 20 years.
(735)

CASEY
See Connolly.
(339)

CASSIDY
Erected by James Cassidy of Bredin St in memory of his father Patrick and his mother Elizabeth. Also his brother Michael who is also here.
(628)

CASSIDY
Erected by Charles Cassidy of Old Hill, Drogheda in memory of his mother Rose Cassidy who departed this life 20th March 1847 aged 67 years. Also his father Charles Cassidy died 18th March 1848 aged 66 years. Also the above Charles who died 23rd October 1849 aged 33 years.
(664)

CAULFIELD
Erected by James Caulfield of Drogheda in memory of his affectionate and dutiful son John Caulfield whom it pleased God to take away in a very short time in the prime of life on the 11th day of August 1832 aged 34 years.
(924)

CAVANAGH
Erected by John Cavanagh of Greenhills in memory of his mother Jane Cavanagh who died 22nd December 1846 aged 79 years.
(176)

CAVANAGH
Pray for the souls of James Cavanagh of Laurence Street Drogheda who died 28th September 1863 and of Patrick his brother who died 9th April 18
(329)

CAVANAGH
Erected by Anne Cavanagh in memory of her father Michael Mackin who died 16th May 185- Also her mother Ellen Mackin who died 24 November 187-.
(423)

CAVANAGH
Erected by Anne Cavanagh of Drogheda in memory of her beloved husband Charles Cavanagh who departed this life 5th February 1825 aged 51 years. Also three of his children who died young. The above named Anne Cavanagh died 8th January 1827 aged 65 years.
(840)

CEGGLY
This stone was erected by Patt Ceggly.
Here lyeth the body of his father John Ceggly who departed this life 20th of January 1761 aged 31 years.

(582)

CHADWICK
M S Joannis Chadwick
Qui annos natis lx. obiit
Die 11 Januarii MDCCCXLI(1841)

Vidua Moerens. Filiique
Lugentes Posueri
Requiescat in pace.

Orate pro Anima Francis ect.
Joannis Chadwick
Viduoe Obiit die nona Julii AD MDCCCXIIX R.I.P. (1899)

Joannis Chadwick natus die 2 Aug 1809
Obiit die 8 Jan 1893,
Cujus animae propitietur Deus
Pater   Ave.

(309)

CHESTER
This Stone was erected to the memory of Michael Chester Esq. of Drogheda by his wife Anne Chester. He departed this life 12th of April 1814.
Also his daughter Rose Ann 21st of December 1809 age 24 years.

(651)

CHESTER
This Stone and Burial Place belongeth to Myles Chester of Drogheda wherein lieth six of his children 1759. Also his wife Rose Chester who died 18th February 1773 age 43 years

(652)

CHESTER
The Burial Place of Myles Chester, Esq. of Drogheda.
Here lieth the body of his wife Anne Chester who died 18th February 1773 aged 43 years.
John Chester third eldest son died 16th February.1768 age 10 years. Also his second wife Eliza Chester who died 2nd day of November 1788. Beneath lieth the body of the above Myles Chester who died 17th February 1794 age 71 years. Here also lieth the body of John Chester eldest son of the above Myles Chester, by his second wife who died 5th day of July 1791 age 19 years. Rose Elizabeth his daughter died October 1803 age 22 years.
(See History of Kilsaran by Rev. James B. Leslie 1908 in which he says: ìthat a monument in Kilsaran Church, to the above Michael Chester, does not tally with the above which states that his mortal remains lie in these sacred precincts and there is a descrepancy in the age) p.300.

CLARE
Erected by Mary A Clare, Scarlet Street, in memory of her father Patrick Clare and her mother Margaret. Also her husband Stephen Clare who died 11th August 1895. Her sister Elizabeth died 1st February 1873.

(526)

CLAIR
See McCann.

(457)

CLARK
This stone was erected by Michael Clarke of Drogheda for him and his family. Here lieth the body of James Clarke his father who died 24th June 1764 aged 70 years. Also four of his children and three of his brothers.

(527)

CLARK
This stone and burial place belongeth to James Clark of Drogheda, herein lieth the body of his daughter Mary who died 6th May 1771 aged 17 years.

(579)

CLARK
This burial place belongeth to Cormick Clark where lies four of his children 1775.
Also of his wife who died 27th June 1781 aged 40 years.

(711)

CLARKE
Katie Clarke of Dowth died 3rd November 1884 aged 27 years.

(139)

CLARKE
Erected to the memory of Elizabeth Clarke, Bolton Street who departed this life on the 22nd of May 1870 aged 55 years and her brother Philip who died 30th November 1861 aged 51 years.

(236)

CLARKE
Erected 1885 by James A. Clarke High Sheriff of Drogheda in memory of his daughter Mary who died 30th August 1870 aged 3 years. His wife Ellen who died 7th June 1872 aged 33 years.
His mother Mrs. Mary Clarke who died 13th February 1883 aged 76 years.
His daughter Mary Angela died 13th June 1883 aged 3 years and Lillie who died 19th August 1884 aged 16 years and Kathleen who died 19th August 1911.
The above names James A. who died 13th December 1919 aged 87 and his wife Margaret who died 11th December 1923 aged 76.
(James A.Clarke, 8 Shop Street, Auctioneer, Valuator, Insurance Commission Agent, was one of those men who went with Fr. James Anderson, to Knock in 1880. While High Sheriff, he was instrumental in founding the GAA in Co. Louth in 1885.)

(344)

CLARKE
Erected by Jane Clarke Bull Ring in memory of her mother Ann Clarke who died 20th September 1899. Also the above Jane Clarke who died 23rd December 1915.
(389)

CLARKE
Erected by Andrew Clarke in memory of his wife Sarah 18th June 1879 aged 50 years.
(460)

CLARKE
Erected by Mary Clarke 21st October 1822 in memory of her husband Owen Clarke

> Honesty was his ambition
> Industry his amusement

And the above Mary Clarke died 27th July 1827.
(520)

CLARKE
Erected by Patrick Clarke of Bolton Street in memory of his son Patrick who died 25th December 1871 aged 12 years.
(788)

CLARKE
Erected by Catherine Clarke in memory of her parents who died at Scarlet Street Drogheda. John Clarke 31st March 1883 aged 80 years, and Mary on 10th July 1886 aged 77 years.
(804)

CLARKE
In memory of Marianne the beloved wife of Eugene Clarke who died 8th October 1860 aged 23 years, also their infant child Eugene and his nephew James C. McCabe late of New York 23rd August 1892.
(937)

CLARKE
See Hand.
(421)

CLIFFORD
Erected by Edward Clifford West Street, Drogheda, in memory of William Scott who died 23rd February 1872, also his sister Margaret who died 12th March 1867 and his sister Mrs. Anne Clifford who died 21st May 1887. His daughter Kate died 5th October 1889, and Mary died 20th January 1891. The above Edward who died 29th October 1920 aged 84 years, his daughter Margaret who died 14th January 1937 also Eugene last surviving son of the above Edward who died 15th May 1938.
(348)

CLINTON
Erected to the memory of Michael Clinton of North Road who died 21st March 1846 aged 37 years.
(39)

CLINTON
Erected by Peter Clinton, John's Gate, in memory of his daughter Mary who died 11th September 1869.

(126)

CLINTON
In memory of Rose Clinton who died 24th May 1873 aged 30 years and her husband William Clinton.

(203a)

CLINTON
Sacred to the memory of Mrs. Jane Clinton wife of William Clinton, Dyer Street. She departed this life 8th of May 1832. Also the above William Clinton died 27th March 1864.

(898)

CLINTON
O Holy Cross under thy shadow will I rest in peace. Of your charity pray for the soul of Bessie the wife of William Clinton. Born 12th October 1842 died 1st February 1876. Beneath are also interred the remains of their son William Robert born 13th December 1873 died 13th February 1876, and four of their infant children. Also Thomas W. died 23rd March 1894 aged 23 years. The following are also interred here Aileen M who died 17th January 1897 aged 18 years, William A died 7th October 1900 aged 20 years. Child of the above William Clinton who died 31st October 1906 aged 59 years.

(346)

CLINTON
See Matthews.

(229)

CLINTON
See Kavanagh.

(264)

CLUSKEY
Erected by Nicholas Cluskey, North King St, Dublin, in memory of his daughter Margaret Mary who died 1st April 1883 aged 13 years, and his son Andrew aged 14 months.

(75)

CLUSKEY
Of your charity pray for the souls of Margaret Cluskey who died 1st January 1888 aged 85 years. Her daughter Mary died 1851 aged 15 years, and her son John who died young. Her husband James died 1848 whose remains lie in The Leck, Rossnaree.

(283)

COFFEY
Owen Coffey and Margaret Morris.

(167)

COFFEY
Erected by M.A. and L. Coffey in memory of their father who died 31st October 1864, their mother and brothers Patrick who are also interred here. Also their sister Margaret who died 2nd January 1888.

(934)

COLGAN
Erected by Patrick Colgan of Yellowbatter in memory of his wife Margaret who departed this life 22nd October 1794 aged 60 years.

(643)

COLLIER
Thomas Collier died 7th March 1873 and Catherine Collier died 5th November 1875.

(295)

COLLEN
Erected A.D. 1820 by Patrick Collen of Drogheda in memory of his father John Collen who departed this life 10th November 1807 aged 62 years. Also Catherine Collen his wife, died 16th July 1849 aged 54 years, and the above Patrick Collen died 6th March 1853 aged 63 years.

(660)

COLLINS
Erected by James Collins, Sandyford Ally, in memory of his father Michael Collins who died 31st May 1863. Also one child who died young.

(68)

COLLINS
Erected by Michael Collins, Dublin Road, in memory of his children. Michael aged 2 and a half years. Lawrence aged 1 year and 6 months died 2nd February 1873. Francis died 29th November 1877 aged 2 months. Teresa Mary died 24th January 1881 aged 2 years. Thomas Paul died 2nd March 1885 aged 2 years and 3 months. Monica Mary died 14th January 1892 aged 4 years and 8 months.

(157)

COLLINS
Erected to the memory of Bartholomew Collins late of Bullring, Drogheda, who died 24th May 1852 and his wife Anne who died 22nd August 1872, and eight of their children who died young.

(182)

COLLINS
In memory of Peter Collins late of Dyer St. who died 16th September 1879 aged 72 years. Erected by his daughter Bridget Collins.

(906)

COLLINS
See Fullam.

(354)

COMERFORD
Erected by Mary Comerford, Ship St. in memory of her mother Bridget who died 15th February 1895 aged 63 years.

(123)

COMERFORD
Erected by Jane Comerford in memory of her husband Michael who died in the year 1858 also her daughter Mary Anne who died young.

(797)

COMMORFORD
Erected by James Commorford of Drogheda in memory of his brother Michael who died 23rd June 1826 aged 27 years.

(891)

CONATY
Erected by Thomas Conaty in memory of his wife Mary who died 19th May 1891 also five of their children who died young.

(202a)

CONN
See Shiels.

(100)

CONNOLLY
Erected by Bridget Connolly of Trinity Street, Drogheda, in memory of her husband Thomas Connolly who died 12th October, 1867. Also her three children Annie, Margaret and Thomas who died young and the above Bridget who died 23rd December 1894 aged 87 years.

(174)

CONNOLLY
Erected by Alderman Thos. Connolly, High Sheriff in memory of his wife Mary who died 9th October, 1871. Also of her mother Margaret Courtney who died 26th October 1877, who was revered for her charity and piety. Her father Barth Courtney who died 13th April 1879 and her brother Joseph who died 16th May 1879, also Mary Agatha daughter of the above Thos, and Mary Connolly who was borne away by the angels in the simplicity of her youth to the realms of peace and happiness 4th January 1880 in the 11th year of her age.

(306)

CONNOLLY
Erected by Mary Connolly in memory of her husband Thos. Connolly, Bullring, Drogheda, who died 27th November 1861, also their son Patrick who died 18th July 1859.

(326)

CONNOLLY
Sacred to the memory of Mr. Patrick Connolly of James Street, Drogheda, who departed this life the 16th January 1847 aged 42 years.
(327)

CONNOLLY
Sacred to the memory of Peter Connolly died 27th July 1872 aged 69 years. Here also are interred the remains of the late Alderman Patrick Casey J.P. died 18th September 1880 aged 76 years. Also Elizabeth Connolly wife of the above who died 18th June 1888 aged 70 years. Also Alderman Patrick Casey Connolly J.P. son of the above Peter & Elizabeth Connolly who died 9th April 1894 aged 41 years.

(339)

CONNOLLY
Erected by James Connolly of Drogheda in memory of his wife Mary who died 2nd December 1867. Pray for the soul of Thomas Connolly of Shop Street who died 25th June 1894 and his son Dr. James J. died 8th April 1920. Also Alice wife of the above Thomas who died 18th January 1928.
(340)

CONNOLLY
Beloved wife Eliza died 9thFebruary 1872. The above John Connolly died 16th November 1885 aged 75 years. (Top part of this stone missing)
(500)

CONNOLLY
See Bannon.
(370)

CONNOLLY
See Dolan.
(393)

CONNOR
Erected by Patrick Connor, Peter St. in memory of his father Michael Connor who died 22nd September 1878 and also his five children who died young. Also his wife Margaret who died 6th April 1885 aged 35 years.
(71)

CONNOR
Erected by Charles Connor of Nuns Walk, in memory of his beloved wife Anne Connor who died 17th September 1875 aged 47 years, also three of their children who died young. The above Charles Connor who died 4th October 1888 aged 65 years.
(146)

CONNOR
Erected by Margaret Connor in memory of her mother Catherine Connor who died 23rd January 1876 aged 70 years. Her brother Patrick died in 1858 and her father Patrick Connor died 17th December 1877 aged 60.
(707)

CONNOR
Erected A.D.1882. Pray for the soul of Bernard and Mary Connor and their children. Thomas Moore grandson of the above who died 18th July 1891 and his daughter Marianna Moore who died 12th December 1899.
(858)

CONNOR
See Byrne.
(406)

COOGAN
Erected by Mrs. Anne Coogan of Cartown in memory of her husband Nicholas Coogan who died on 17th July 1888 aged 73 years.
(215)

COOGAN
Erected by Nicholas Coogan in memory of his wife who died 24th November 1886.

(645)

COOKE
Mary Cooke of Platten Road, her father John Cooke and family.

(223)

COONEY
Erected by James Cooney late Chief Officer, R.N. in memory of his wife Eliza who died 30th July 1890 aged 71 years. His beloved mother Mary who died 15th September 1877 aged 84 years. His sister Maria who died 19th March 1859 aged 36 years. His brother Capt. John Cooney U.S. Army shot in California about 27th May 1854 aged 35 years. Also the above James who died 3rd July 1908 aged 85 years.

(319)

COONEY
Erected by Owen Cooney, Dale, Drogheda, in memory of his son Owen Francis who died 2nd January 1871 aged 6 months. Also his son Michael John died 1st September 1872 aged 9 months. His daughter Catherine died 16th December 1872 aged 6 years.

(468)

COONEY
Erected by Thomas Cooney Colph in memory of his mother Judith Cooney who died 30th April 1862 aged 60 years.

(706a)

COONEY
See Byrne.

(501)

COOTE
Of your charity pray for the soul of Edward Coote who died 22nd April 1855 aged 54. Also his wife Rose who died 18th March 1857 aged 52 years. Their son Charles died 29th June 1857 aged 23 years.

(97)

COOTE
Erected by Bridget Coote in memory of her husband Thomas Coote who died 13th December 1880, and her daughter Bridget who died 18th December 1873.

(98)

CORCORAN
Erected by John Corcoran, Dublin Road, in memory of his sons Laurence who died 2nd November 1879 aged 3 years and Mathew and James who died 21st October 1892 aged 21 years.

(237)

CORCORAN
See Cunningham.

(200)
CORNYN
In memory of Sergeant James Cornyn R.I.C. Cord Road, died 16th March 1891 aged 49 years.

(260)
CORRIGAN
A.D.1872 Erected by Patrick Corrigan, Scarlet Street, in the memory of his son Patrick who died 9th December 1862. Also his beloved wife Mary who died 11th November 1870, the above Patrick Corrigan who died 26th February 1875.

(113)
CORRIGAN
See Hand.

(269)
CORRIGAN
See Campbell.

(391)
CORRY
Erected by Thomas Corry of Drogheda.

(488)
COSTELLO
In memory of Michael Costello, Stockwell Lane.

(443)
COSTELLO
In memory of our father and mother John and Anne Costello, Peter St.

(444)
COSTIGAN
Erected by Denis Costigan in memory of his wife Ann Costigan who died 4th September 1849 aged 38 years. Requiescant in peace Amen.

(43)
COTTOR
Erected by Margaret Cottor, Cord Road, in memory of her mother who died 14th May 1874 aged 82 years.

(50)
COYEL
Here lieth the body of Patrick Coyel who died anno 1771 aged 60 years.

(642)
COYLE
In memory of James Coyle, Magdalene St. died 20th August 1894, his wife Alice died 5th June 1899, and their four children Peter, James, Christopher and Alice also Mary and Margaret Coyle.

(455)

COYLE
Erected by Elizabeth Coyle of Scarlet Street in memory of her parents James and Mary Coyle, and her brothers John and James and Patrick and her sisters Alice and Mary.

(780)

COURTENEY
Erected by Mr. Patrick Courteney of West Street in memory of his son Joseph who died 24th October 1855 aged 17 years. Also his daughter Teresa Maria who died 17th January 1864 aged 10 years. Here also are interred the remains of Jane relict of the above Patrick Courteney who died 12th January 1895 aged 85 years. Here lieth also the remains of Anne Tierney the faithful servant of the family who died 8th May 1890.

(627)

COURTNEY
Erected by Patrick Courtney in memory of his children Patrick, Marianne, John Henry, Patrick Alphonsus and Bartholomew all who died young.

(332)

COURTNEY
Erected by George Courtney of Drogheda to the memory of his nephew James Gibson who died 21st November 1852 aged 3 years. Also John and Margaret Courtney, brother and sister of George Courtney, who died young.

(657)

COURTNEY
See Connolly.

(306)

CRAWFORD
Erected by Elizabeth Crawford of the Marsh in memory of her husband John who died 5th September 1886 aged 60 years.

(251)

CREAVEN
Erected by Michael Creaven of Dublin Gate, Drogheda, in memory of his father Brian who died 23rd February 1845 aged 65 years.

(730)

CRILLY
Erected 1886 by Andrew Joseph Crilly in memory of his children Andrew, Joseph, William, Patrick and Catherine who died young.

(784)

CRINION
Erected by Thomas Crinion in memory of his mother Anne Crinion who died 4th April 1877 aged 54 years.

(925)

CRINION
See Walsh.
(706)

CRUISE
Erected by Anne Cruise in memory of her husband Patrick Cruise who died 21st April 1882 aged 64 years. His daughter Margaret died 11th September 1870 aged 19 years. And his other daughter Mary died 5th August 1882.
(896)

CULLEN
1769. This stone and burial place belongeth to Martin Cullen and his posterity, wherein lieth three of his children.
(612)

CULLEN
Here lies Martin Cullen of Drogheda, Merchant, who died 29th May 1783 aged 60 years, also seven of his children. Also his wife Alice died 26th December 1784 aged 56 years.
(613)

CULLODEN
See Reilly.
(779)

CUMMINS
Of your charity pray for the repose of the soul of Mrs. Winifred Mary Cummins (alias Blake) who died 8th October 1891.
(396)

CUMMISKEY
Pray for the soul of Anne Cummiskey who died 26th May 1877.
(954)

CUNNINGHAM
Erected by Catherine Cunningham of the Dale, in memory of her father James Cunningham who died 30th April 1865. Also her mother Bridget Cunningham who died in Holyoke, U.S.A.
(106)

CUNNINGHAM
Erected by Annie Cunningham A.D. 1806 in memory of her father and mother Thomas and Annie Corcoran and two of her children who died young.
(200)

CUNNINGHAM
Erected by Rose Cunningham of Jewett City, Conn. U.S.A. in memory of her daughter Anne who died 23rd September 1879 aged 23 years, and her son Joseph who died young.
(425)

CUNNINGHAM
Henry Cunningham died 29th July 1849.
(729)

CURRAN
Catherine Curran of Platten died 20th December 1882 aged 80 years.

(392)

CURRAN
See Dodd.

(322)

CURIN
This stone was erected by Patt Curin of Drogheda and his posterity and here lies numbers of his friends.

(712)

CURLEY
Erected A.D. 1862 by Judith Curley, James St. in memory of her husband Michael Curley who died February 1856. Also her son Augustine who died young. And her son James Curley who died 19th February 1890 aged 35 years.

(708)

CURLEY
See Kelly.

(427)

CURRY
Erected by Anne Curry of Trinity Street, Drogheda, as a tribute of respect to the memory of her husband Mathew Curry, who departed this life 22nd July 1849 aged 55 years. Also her daughter Bridget deceased 17th July 1849 aged 16 years, and her son Mat who died young. Also John 14th June 1852 in the 11th year of his age. The above Anne Curry died 19th December 1864 aged 66 years and son James died 8th January 1868 aged 31 years.

(240)

CURTIS
Erected by James Curtis of Peter Street, Drogheda, in memory of his father Thomas Curtis who died 27th August 1825 aged 70 years. Also his mother Mary Curtis died 30th March 1836 aged 76 years, and his daughter Mary who died young. And also his wife Mary, 9th November 1865 aged 60 years and the above James Curtis died 4th March 1868 aged 78 years. Two infant children of James son of the above James Curtis, and his wife Annie who died 8th March 1880 aged 34 years, and of his brother Thomas who died the 7th May 1888 aged 54 years.

(44)

CUSACK
See Pickett.

(72)

DALTON
Erected by Catherine Dalton in memory of her beloved husband Thomas Dalton of Drogheda. Carpenter who departed this left 28th November 1813 aged 70 years. Many of his ancestors are also

(ESTABLISHED 1867.)

IT IS UNIVERSALLY ADMITTED
THAT THE BEST VALUE IN GROCERIES
IS TO BE HAD AT

THOMAS DALY'S,
SHOP STREET,
DROGHEDA
(Next the Augustinian Church).

TEAS.

PURE ASSAM, HIGHEST PRICE		2s. 8d. per lb.
EXCELLENT BLENDED TEAS,		2s. 0d. ,, ,,
USEFUL MIXED	Do.	1s. 8d. ,, ,,

WINES. SANDEMAN'S Fine Crusted Port, 10 Years in Bottle. SHERRIES, Pale and Golden, MARSALA, Pure and Genuine. CLARET, at every Price from 12s.

WHISKEY. A Large Stock of JOHN JAMESON & SON'S SIX YEARS OLD; the same Genuine quality which has heretofore given such general satisfaction.

BASS & CO.'S PALE ALE, in Sparkling condition; GUINNESS'S PURE DOUBLE STOUT; DROGHEDA ALE; JAMES HENNESSY'S 10 YEARS' OLD BRANDY in Wood and Flask.

THOMAS DALY,
Wholesale & Retail Grocer,
WINE AND SPIRIT MERCHANT,
SHOP STREET, DROGHEDA.

Advertisement for Thomas Daly. Bassett's Louth 1886.

here interred. Here also are interred the above Catherine Dalton who died 4th January 1820 aged 58 years. Also her daughter Ellen Dalton who died 16th October 1853 aged 68 years.

(819)

DALY
In memory of Mary wife of Bernard Daly, Bolton Street, Drogheda, who died 5th April 1875 aged 57 years, and the above Bernard died 24th May 1911 aged 95 years, and his son Gerald died 25th June 1924 aged 74 years. Also Elizabeth Dolan relict of Gerald died 4th November 1952. R.I.P.

(356)

DALY
Erected by Thomas Daly, Shop Street, in memory of his sister Mary Flood died 13th July 1888. O Sacred Heart of Jesus have Mercy on her and the above Thomas Daly died 22nd September 1913 aged 83 years. And his niece Rosanna died 12th March 1917 also Mary wife of Michael Daly, Shop Street, died 17th April 1917. Miss Mary Tyrrell died 30th September 1959 and the above Michael Daly died 27th May 1965.

(366)

(An advertisement for Thomas Daly, Wholesale and Retail Grocer, Wine and Spirit Merchant, 36 Shop Street. has "established in 1867". It continued from him to his son, Michael Daly and to his son Louis, until the business was sold in 1979).

No. 36 Shop Street, Michael Daly and a friend with his daughter Carmel (Mrs. Dwyer) and his son Louis. Courtesy Paddy Dwyer.

DALY
This tomb was erected by Robert Daly of Drogheda, Merchant, to the memory of his wife Marianne who died 16th May 1832 aged 42 years. His son Joseph 6th August 1831 age 11 years. Here also is the above Robert Daly who died 6th February 1836 aged 85 years. His son Charles 3rd September 1864 aged 41 years. His son Robert 8th August 1867 aged 43 years. His last surviving son Thomas is also interred here who entered into rest on 28th January 1888 aged 63 years.

(665)

DARDIS
This is the burial place of John Dardis wherein lieth his wife Mary Dardis who departed this life 18th July 1776 aged 58 years. Also six of his children R.I.P.

(675)

DAUM
A tribute of respect by Catherine Daum to the memory of her beloved companion Joseph Daum who departed this life 17th May 1843 aged 80 years. Also his former companion Ann Daum who died 4th January 1831.

(861)

DAW
Erected by John Daw, James Street, Drogheda, in memory of his father and mother also three of his children who died young. The above John Daw died 29th November 1868, his wife Bridget died 7th January 1869, their son Patrick died 27th July 1871 aged 27 years.

(73)

DEAN
Erected by Thomas Dean of Laytown in memory of his mother and sister Eliza and Anne Dean.

(285)

DEAZ
This stone and burial place belongeth to Thomas Deaz of the Town of Drogheda, Taylor, wherein lieth the body of his wife Anne Deaz who departed this life 30th June 1769 aged 34 years. Also six of his children. And Thomas Deaz died 16th July 1778 aged 42 years.

(654)

DEERY
Erected by Michael Deery in memory of his daughter Mary Anne Deery who died 7th March 1890 in the 11 year of her age. The above Michael Deery died 21st February 1907. Kathleen his daughter died 8th January 1923. Mary wife of the above Michael died 12th February 1929.

(409)

DELANEY
Pray for the soul of Daniel Delaney who died 2nd March 1874.

(203)

DENNIS
Erected by James Dennis, West Street, in memory of his wife Mary Anne who died 13th December 1877 aged 29 years.

(325)

DEVIN
Erected by Denis Devin of Drogheda in memory of his mother Margaret Devin who departed this life the 25th of August 1842 aged 75 years. Also his brother Andrew died 5th January. 1849 aged 18 years. Also the above Denis died 10th October 1849 aged 43 years and Eliza wife of Denis Devin who died on Easter Sunday 12th April 1892 aged 76 years. A good Mother mourned by her children.

(261)

DEVIN
Have Mercy O Lord on the soul of John and Bridget Devin, Newfoundwell, Drogheda. Their children, Rose, John Joseph and William Thomas and John Bernard infant son of James Devin Dublin. Also their son Pat Devin who died 4th July 1883.
(351)

DEVIN
This stone was erected 1799 by Paul Devin of Drogheda. Here lieth the body of his father-in-law James Keenan who departed this life 19th January 1774 aged 43 years. His wife also Catherine Keenan and their son John Keenan their daughter Mary died 27th October 1797.
(589)

DEVIN
4TH June 1888, at the residence of her brother-in-law, Thomas Brady, Esq., TC., West Street, Drogheda. Mrs. Kate Devin, sister of Michael Finegan, Esq.,TC.,John Street. Interment took place in the Cord Cemetery on Tuesday last.   (Death Insertion, *Dundalk Democrat*. 7th June 1888).

DEVIN
Erected A.D. 1809 by Patrick Devin of Drogheda in memory of his wife Jane who died 11th December 1808 age 84 years. Also his son Laurence Devin who died 12th March 1832 aged 20 years.
(673)

DEVIN
Erected by Patrick Devin in memory of his father Nicholas Devin who departed this life the 22nd April 1822 aged 45 years. Also his sister Margaret Devitt who died 3rd November 1827 aged 26 years and his mother Anne Devin died 24th October 1845 aged 64 years.
(950)

DEVIN
See Finegan.
(6)

DEVIN
See Gogarty.
(18)

DEVINE
Erected by James Devine in memory of his wife Mary Devine departed this life 31st January 1837 aged 55 years.
(908)

DEVITT
Erected by John Devitt, Peter Street, Drogheda, in memory of his father Thomas Devitt who died 10th August 1849 aged 44 years. Also his wife Anne who died 1st August 1863 aged 32 years. Also his daughter Rose Anne who died young.
(740)

DEVITT
See Devin.

(950)

DEVLIN
Luke Devlin. (Rough uncut stone 15" high).

(78)

DEVLIN
Erected by Thomas Devlin, Patrick Street, in memory of his brother Luke 1865.

(79)

DIDMOND
The family grave of William Didmond of Tubberboice.

(865)

DIVIN
This stone and burial place belongeth to James Divin of Drogheda who departed this life the 10th May 1782 aged 60 years and five of his children. Also Mary his wife who died the 5th May 1792 aged 80 years.

(817)

P.J. Dodd of Drogheda, Architect & Civil Engineer.

DODD
Erected by Mrs. P.J. Dodd, Peter Street, in memory of her mother Mrs. Margaret Curran who died 21st March 1886, also her husband P.J. Dodd who died 19th January 1892.

(322)

(Dodd was only 47 years of age when he died. A noted architect of the day, among his many commissions were, the Mortuary Chapel in the Cord Cemetery, St. Mary's Church, James Street, Donecarney School, Mercy Convent, Dublin Road and the Whitworth Monument).

DOLAN
Erected by Philip A. Dolan in memory of his mother Mary Dolan who died 25th January 1938 and his grandmother Eliza Connolly who died 12th March 1903. The above Philip who died 7th December 1966.

(393)

DOLAN
Sacred to the memory of John Dolan of Beleek, Co. Fermanagh, who accidentally drowned in the River Boyne at Drogheda, 11th August 1877 aged 22 years. May he rest in peace.

(287)

DOLAN
In loving memory of James Dolan. Laurence Street, who died 18th July 1912, his wife Elizabeth died 9th September 1908, their daughter Mary Bridget died 19th April 1912, their son John died 29th November 1902. Also his brother John died 13th December 1914, his brother Owen Dolan who died 24th November 1929 and interred in St. Peters Cemetery.

(428)

DOLAN
In memory of Philip Dolan of Termonfeckin, 9th February 1874 aged 63 years and his wife Bridget who died 6th March 1877 aged 64 years.

(795)

DOLAN
Erected by Patrick Dolan, Bredin Street, in memory of his brother William died 6th April 1861. Also his brother Laurence died 11th February 1862. Also the above named Patrick Dolan died 27th April 1865 and his sister Mary died 2nd March 1874.

(796)

DOLLARD
This stone marks the spot where the mortal remains of Bridget the beloved wife of Patrick Dollard of Drogheda are interred. She departed this life 20th August 1847. It is also commemorative of the father of Patrick Dollard, James, aged 90 who died 18th March 1848.

(20)

DOMINICAN NUNS
This stone and burial place belongs to the Dominican Nuns of Drogheda 1792. Requiescant in peace.
(This stone was not seen; the above is taken from Hughes History.........
An enquiry to Sr. M. Thomas OP> Archivist, Sienna Convent, in 1975 had the following answer.
"As regards the Cord, the inscription, as given in Hughes History, is complete. There was no names on that stone or anywhere in the Cord. The Exhumation took place in 1972. The remains, in two coffins, were brought here in the evening of July 27th and buried in our cemetery after Mass on July 28th 1972. The stone is now flat on top of the ground".)

The Dominican Nuns' Stone from the Cord, now lying flat in the centre of the Siena Graveyard, Cord Road, has a new stone with the following inscription.........

> "In the 250th year from the foundation of this monastery, the remains of
> its venerated foundress, Mother M. Catherine Plunkett, together with those
> of the Nuns deceased previous to AD 1818, which formerly rested beneath
> this stone in the Cord Cemetery, were re-interred here on 28th July AD 1972."

DONAGAN
Erected by Matthew Donagan in memory of his mother Anne Donagan who died 18th November 1858.

(55)

DONEGAN
Erected by Patrick and Kate Donegan of Bray, Co. Wicklow and late of Laurence Street, Drogheda, in memory of two of their children died young. The above Patrick died 26th August 1925 aged 72 and Kate died 6th December 1942 aged 74.

(384)

DOUGHEAN
This stone and burial place belongeth to Patrick Doughean, cord-winder of Drogheda and his posterity Y 1771. (There are no more words on this stone).

(279)

DOUNEY
This stone was erected by Christopher Douney. Underneath lieth the body of his father Thomas Douney who died January 1769 aged 78 years.

(540)

DOWD
Erected by Peter Dowd, Mossley, Belfast, in memory of his wife Eliza who died 5th March 1874. Also of his children Robert, Joseph, Judith, Amelia, Peter and Anselm whose remains are herein interred.

(410)

Advertisement for John Dowd's Bee-hive Bar from Drogheda Civic Week Programme 1938.

DOWD
Erected by John Dowd, Laurence Street, in memory of his sister Annie Kavanagh who died 18th March 1904, his father Patrick died 7th December 1911 and his mother Mary died 8th December 1917 and the above John died 8th April 1957 and his wife Annie

(434)

DOWD
See Byrne.

(406)

DOWDALL
> Beneath This Stone there lyeth One
> That still his Friends did please
> To Heaven I hope hes surely gone
> To enjoy Eternal Ease.

Here lyeth the body of John Dowdall who departed this life the 16th Day of October 1778 in the 29th year of his age. Of your charity pray for the soul of Anne wife of Arthur Quinn who died 5th April 1879 in her 74 year. And of Arthur Quinn who died 4th May 1886 in his 80th year. Both of whom died at Liverpool and were interred here.

(518)

DOWDALL
See Verdon.

(503)

DOYLE
Erected by Thomas Doyle of William Street, Drogheda, to the memory of his sister Honoria Doyle died AD 1846 and his six children who died young. Also Elizabeth Doyle his wife died 12th May AD 1850 aged 40 years.

(92)

DOYLE
Have mercy o Lord on the soul of Anne Doyle who died AD 1862. Also her husband Richard Doyle who died 17th August 1888.

(583)

DOYLE
See Odair.
(140)

DREW
In memory of Anthony Drew of John Street who died April 1863. And his wife Rose April 1883 and their family interred here.
(40)

DREW
Erected by Lawrence Drew, Crooked Street, in memory of his son Lawrence who died young 29th April 1862.
(89)

DRUMGOOLE
This burial place belongeth to James Drumgoole wherein lieth his mother Mary Drumgoole who died 7th August 1770 aged 55 years.
(618)

DUFF
Erected by Peter Duff in memory of his wife Catherine who died 24th April 1881 aged 50 years.
(825)

DUFFY
Gloria in excelsis Deo
Erected AD 1853 by Owen Duffy of Trinity Street, Drogheda, in memory of his honoured mother Mrs. Judith Duffy of the Old Hill who died on the 10th February 1853 aged 76 years also John Duffy relict if the above Mrs. Duffy who died the 22nd May 1856 aged 83 years and the above Owen Duffy who died 19th June 1867 aged 57 years.
(34)

DUFFY
Jane wife of John Duffy died 23rd January 1903 (A coffin in the vault).

DUFFY
Pray for the soul of John Duffy who died 22nd November 1885 aged 75 years. Erected by his daughter Rose Anne.
(494)

DUFFY
Erected AD 1810 by Mr. Angis Duffy of Drogheda in memory of his wife Ann Duffy alias Bath who died 25th October 1810 age 36 years. Also his son Bernard died 24th April 1876 age 73 years.
(684)

DUFFY
In memory of Elizabeth wife of James Duffy, Windmill Lane, who died 23rd December 1878.
(785)

DUFFY
Erected AD 1838 by Catherine Duffy of West Street, Drogheda, in memory of her beloved husband James Duffy who died 22nd April 1857 aged 48 years. Also her mother Bridget Rodgers who died 17th January 1858 aged 78 years.

(905)

DUFFY
Erected by Mary Duffy of Drogheda in memory of her sister Alice Duffy who died 18th August 1832 aged 21 years.

(905)

DUFFY
See Sisters of Charity.

(1)

DULLAGHAN
Erected by Catherine Dullaghan, Mary Street, to her beloved husband Thomas Dullaghan who died 17th March 1876 aged 84 years, and the above Catherine died 22nd February 1883 and her son Michael died 28th August 1887.

(205a)

DULLAGHAN
See Long.

(64)

DULLAHAN
See Owens.

(275)

DUNLEAVY
Erected by Mrs. Mary Dunleavy in memory of her Aunt Kate McKenna who died on the 14th February 1895 at North Road, Drogheda. Thy will be Done.

(360)

DUNNE
See Smith.

(846)

DUNN
In memory of Mrs.M. Dunn who died 4th April 1898. Rest in peace.

(451)

DURNIN
Erected by Mary Durnin of James Street in memory of her husband Bernard Durnin who died 25th February 1877 aged 74 years and two of their children who died young, and the above Mary Durnin died 26th January 1879.

(153)

DURNIN
Erected in memory of his mother Mary A. Durnin of Patrick Street, who died 5th June 1886 age 60 years. Also his brother Daniel died 29th October 1873 and his sister Kate who died young.
(623)

EADES
Erected by David Eades, Nuns Walk, in memory of his wife Margaret who died 28th June 1866 and the above David died 1st May 1878 aged 72 years.
(185)

EARLY
See Farrell.
(320)

EGAN
See Reid.
(172)

EKINS
Pray for the soul of Dr. Patrick W. Ekins, Colpe, who died August 8th 1876. Anne E. his mother died 7th October 1876, his sister Mary died 9th August 1879, his brother John died 10th March 1880 and his brother Joseph died 4th October 1880
(364)

ELCOCK
See Lowthe.

ELLIOTT
Erected by John Elliott, North Road, in memory of his son Thomas 1883.
(524)

EVERITT
Erected AD 1833 by James Everitt in memory of his wife Catherine who died 9th July 1832 aged 60 years.
(671)

FAGAN
Erected by Julia Fagan in memory of her husband Michael Fagan who died 9th January 1875 aged 53 years. Also their five children who died young and his father Michael died 20th January 1848 aged 58 years.
(747)

FALCONER
Erected AD 186 by Catherine Falconer alias Rafferty of Drogheda in memory of her son Michael Falconer who died 11th May 1820 aged 47 years.
(860)

FALLON
See Miller.

(315)

FARLEY
Erected by Henry Farley in memory of his wife Rebecca who died 11th July 1849 and two of his children who died young.

(726)

FARREL
Erected by Michael Farrel in memory of his father Patrick who died 1822 aged 50 years. And his mother Elizabeth died 1842 aged 70 years.

(262)

FARRELL
Erected by Peter Farrell of Drogheda in memory of his mother Catherine who died 29th July 1849 aged 65 years.

(252)

FARRELL
In memory of Robert Farrell who died on the 2nd March 1842 aged 42 years. Mary, his sister, honouring his virtues and bewailing their loss, has erected this humble stone. His life fulfilled the Procepst of the Religion he professed, the love of God and his neighbour. May God have mercy on his soul. Also the above Mary Farrell who died 20th November 1843 aged 48 years. Also Elizabeth the beloved wife of Michael Early of Nicholls Bridge, Drogheda, who died 28th April 1851 aged 68 years.

(320)

FARRELL
In memory of Eliza Farrell who died 22nd May 1891 aged 61 years and her husband James who died 21st October 1904 aged 78 years.

(461)

FARRELL
Erected by Patrick Farrell, Legavoren, in memory of his father Michael Farrell who died 16th June 1877 aged 62 years. Also his wife Julia who died 18th July 1849 aged 30 years. Also his sister Elizabeth died 22nd September 1874 aged 28 years.

(535)

FARRELL
This stone was erected on the 4th May 1796 by Patrick Farrell of Drogheda. Taylor. Here lyeth four of his children.

(608)

FARRELL
Erected by John Farrell, Laurence Street, in memory of his wife Mary who died on 20th May 1884 and of their children who died young. Also interred are the remains of his parents Andrew and Catherine Farrell of Mell. And the above named John Farrell who died on the 17th December 1886 aged 66 years and of his grand-daughter Mary Butterly.

(850)

The Cord Cemetery

Paddle Steamers 'Kathleen Mavoureen' and 'Colleen Bawn' docked at the Quayside, Drogheda c 1900. Most of the Sea Captains buried in the Cord commanded ships like these on the Drogheda-Liverpool route for the Drogheda Steampacket Company.

FARRELL
Erected 1882 by Rose Farrell, William Street, in memory of her father and mother James and Bridget Smith and sisters Mary and Bridget, also her sons John and Patrick.

(915)

FARRELL
See Byrne.

(199)

FARRELL
See Brogan.

(439)

FARRELL
See Hone.

(447)

FARRELLY
Erected by Mrs. Ellen Farrelly in memory of her dearly beloved husband Mr. Patrick Farrelly of Dublin Road, Drogheda, who departed this lift 6th August 1874 aged 55 years.

(11)

FAULKNER
Erected by Ellen Faulkner, Cord Road, in memory of her mother, also her grandmother and grandfather Mary and Michael Matthews and her sister Mary.

(284)

FAULKNER
Erected by Ellen Faulkner, Cord Road, Drogheda, in memory of her son Bernard who died in Dungarven 28th March 1896. And her son James died 29th April 1901. The above Ellen died 7th April 1907 and her daughter Kate who died young.

(414)

FAY
Sacred to the memory of Captain James Fay, 54 Scarlet Street, who died 21st September 1891, his wife Mary died 13th October 1886 and three sons drowned at sea, Patrick, James and Joseph. His daughter Mary Freeman died 17th October 1906, his daughter-in-law Elizabeth Fay died 29th June 1894, and his grand-daughter Angela May Fay died 11th July 1895.

(375)

FAY
The family burial place of Captain James Fay and posterity. Three sons that was drowned at sea, but no buoy or beacon marks their graves. They lie beneath the waves. And the sweet flowers that deck the spring, bloom on my peaceful grave.

(376)

FAY
Erected by John Fay in memory of his two infant children and his wife Mary Anne who died 13th July 1890 aged 49 years.

(771)

FAY
See Branigan.
(330)

FEE
This stone and burial place belongeth to John Fee wherein lieth his wife and three of his children 1755.
(719)

FEGAN
Erected by Joseph Fegan of Drogheda, a Tanner, in memory of his wife Anne Fegan who departed this life 10th August 1795 aged 80 years, and also his son Nicholas Fegan who died 24th August 1802 aged 4 years.
(768)

FERRALL
Erected by Charles Ferrall in memory of his father Owen Ferrall who died 24th August 1815 aged 66 years and his mother Mary who died 15th September 1815 aged 56 years.
(202)

FINEGAN
Erected by Michael Finegan of John Street, in memory of his father Michael Finegan who departed this life the 28th October 1868 aged 80 years, and also his mother Anne Finegan who died the 30th April 1878 aged 68 years and of his sister Mary Anne Finegan who departed this life 8th August 1886 aged 60 years. Also his sister Mrs. Catherine Devin who died 1st June 1888 aged 56 years, and also the above named Michael Finegan who died 13th March 1889 aged 68 years.
(6)

FINEGAN
In memory of Thomas Finegan, Trinity Street, who died 25th July 1894 aged 46 years.
(233)

FINEGAN
Erected by Philip Finegan to his two sons, John who died 30th June aged 20 years and Michael who died 8th October aged 14 years. (No year of death given).
(291)

FINEGAN
Erected by Patrick Finegan, Georges Street, Drogheda, in memory of his son Philip who died 10th October 1876 aged 28 years. Also his beloved wife Bridget who died 22nd August 1881 aged 65 years. His aunt Maria Finegan died October 1877 aged 60 years. And the above Patrick Finegan who died 24th August 1887 aged 73 years. Also his sons James who died at Balbriggan 9th February 1893 aged 56 years, and Patrick who died 7th February 1906 aged 67 years. Also John who died 29th January 1917 and his grandson Patrick who died 11th October 1921. Also Margaret wife of the above named James, died 1st September 1926 and Margaret J. wife of the above Patrick Finegan Jun, who died 6th May 1932.
(363)

FINEGAN
May Jesus give eternal rest to the soul of James Finegan, 6 Shop Street, who died 24th June 1889 aged 57 years. Erected by his wife Mary, also in memory of their children Thomas, James, Josephine, Mary and Annie who died young. The above Mary Finegan who died 7th March 1919. Also her son Thomas Joseph Finegan who died 3rd March 1934. R.I.P.

(473)

FINEGAN
This stone was erected by Annie Finegan for her husband John Finegan who died 3rd May 1774 aged 36, also three of their children.

(615)

FINEGAN
See Greene.

(523)

FINGLAS
Erected by Mary Finglas of Cooley Bridge, in memory of her husband James who departed this life 18th June 1846 aged 52 years. Also her son John who departed this life 5th May 1850 aged 9 years and her son Matthew who died 8th October 1851 aged 6 years, and Patrick who died young.

(814)

FINGLAS
Erected by Bernard Finglas, Francis Street, Drogheda, in memory of his beloved father, Bryan Finglas who departed this life 14th January 1869 aged 67 years. Also his mother Catherine who died 31st March 1876 aged 72 years.

(815)

FINGLAS
Erected by John Finglas in loving memory of his mother Margaret who died 11th May 1869 and of his brother Bernard who died in Australia. Patrick died in America also John, Peter, Laurence and Stephen

(816)

FINIGAN
This stone was erected by William Finigan of ye City of Dublin, Baker, in memory of his father Patrick who died 3rd March 1751 aged 65 years. May he rest in peace.

(489)

FINNEGAN
See Kelly.

(523)

FITZGERALD
Erected AD 1850 by Edward Fitzgerald, North Quay, Drogheda, in memory of his beloved wife Barbara who died 20th January 1850 aged 35 years. Also five of his children who died young. The above named Edward Fitzgerald died 27th May 1885 aged 74 years.

(746)

FITZMAURICE
Erected by Joseph Fitzmaurice, West Street, in memory of his daughter Mary who died 10th January 1850 aged 7 years and 3 months.

(230)

FITZPATRICK
Erected by Mary Fitzpatrick in memory of her mother Bridget who died 5th July 1845. Also her brother James Fitzpatrick who died in America in 1855, and her sisters Julia, Bridget, Catherine and Anne who are interred here.

(53)

FITZPATRICK
Bridget Fitzpatrick who departed this life the 25th July 1845.

(54)

FITZPATRICK
Erected by Thomas Fitzpatrick of Scarlet Street, in memory of his father and mother Peter and Bridget Fitzsimons. The former died 1844 and the latter 1834.

(773)

FITZSIMONS
This stone was erected by James Fitzsimons, Merchant of Drogheda, for himself and his family. Here lieth four of his children, viz. Bridget, Thomas, Christopher and James 1790. Also his daughter Bridget who died 3rd January 1793 aged 2 years. Mrs. Jane Fitzsimons otherwise Reilly, wife of the above James Fitzsimons who died 23rd September 1795 aged 43.

(775)

FITZSIMONS
Erected by Alice Fitzsimons in memory of her husband Daniel Fitzsimons who died 5th January 1816 aged 50 years. Also her son Thomas, 2nd November 1834 aged 23 years.

(791)

FITZSIMONS
See Bowen.

(790)

FLANAGAN
In memory of Mathew Flanagan, Kellys Lane, who died 8th August 1890 aged 52 years and his eldest son Patrick who died in New York 7th April 1893 aged 23. Also three children who died young. His daughter Kathleen died 12th July 1899 aged 13 and his wife Mary 6th June 1901 aged 58. Also his son James who died 28th April 1902 aged 22. His mother-in-law Bridget Whitehead died 29th September 1904. His son Thomas died 22nd November 1912 aged 35. Anne Whitehead died 11th October 1924 aged 70. John died 25th September 1931 aged 61. His eldest daughter Margaret died 3rd August 1940 and their son Matthew died 1st November 1958 aged 84.

(453)

FLANAGAN
See Whitehead.
(637)

FLEMIN
Patrick Flemin and his wife Margaret who died May 1882 aged 65 years. Also Mary Magill died 5th July 1877 aged 40 years
(787)

FLINN
Erected by Peter Flinn of Magdalene Street, in memory of his wife Mary Flinn who died 26th January 1856. Here also lie the remains of the above named Peter Flinn who died 12th May 1858 aged 61 years.
(24)

FLINN
This stone was erected by Mr. Nicholas Flinn of Drogheda, Merchant. Underneath are interred three of his children and his brother Mr. John Flinn. Here also is Mr. Patrick Flinn late of West Street and son of the above who died 1st August 1858 aged 87 years. Also the above Nicholas Flinn who died 20th September 1878 aged 56 years. This stone was renewed by his wife Mrs. Mary Flinn in 1879.
(552)

FLINN
John Flinn who died 18th August 1811. (A badly worn stone).
(649)

FLOOD
Erected by Thomas and Maryanne Flood in memory of her grandmother Margaret McManus who died June 1886 aged 87 years.
(243)

FLOOD
Erected by John Flood in memory of his father James Flood of Drogheda died 16th March 1841.
(317)

FLOOD
Erected by Mary Anne Flood in memory of her husband Bernard Flood, West Street, Drogheda, who departed this life 5th January 1884.
(341)

FLOOD
See Daly.
(366)

FLYN
See Levins.
(721)

FORSTALL
See Murtagh.
(187)

FOSKEY
See Murphy.
(415)

FOX
Erected by Mary Fox in memory of her dear father Patrick Fox who died 12th April 1876.
(254)

FOX
Sacred to the memory of Anne, wife of Owen Fox of Fair Street, who died 30th September 1884 and of their children who died young. Also of his father Thomas, who died 27th May 1898 and their son Thomas died 18th May 1907.
(438)

FOX
Erected by Mrs. Margaret Fox, Bolton Street, in memory of her husband Michael Fox who departed this life 1st August 1877 aged 70 years.
(830)

FOX
Erected by John Fox of Laurence Gate in memory of his mother Mary Fox who died 16th June 1848 aged 48 years.
(853)

FREEMAN
See Fay.
(375)

FRITH
Erected by Richard Frith in memory of his wife Margaret Frith who died 23rd October 1862, and his child Peter Frith who died in October 1859. Also to the memory of his father-in-law Peter McCann who died 9th June 1844, and his mother in law Mary McCann died 11th January 1868. Also his son Richard who was killed on the Great Northern Railway 9th July 1882.
(716)

FULLAM
Erected by Mary Fullam, Beltichburn, Drogheda, in memory of her brother Patrick Healy who died 24th August 1898 and her sister Bridget Collins who died 9th March 1900, also the above Mary Fullam who died 18th November 1900. Ellen Martin died 16th December 1908 and her nephew Thomas Collins who died 26th August 1926. Also his wife Mary Collins who died 6th June 1932.
(354)

GAFFNEY
Erected by John Gaffney of Athcarne, in memory of his mother-in-law Mary Walsh who died 16th September 1886 aged 72 years.
(231)

GAHAGAN
See Gaynor.

(744)

GALLAGHER
In sad and loving memory of devoted parents Michael Stephen Gallagher who died 16th April 1860 and his wife Teresa the 18th October 1891.
On whose souls sweet Jesus have mercy.
Our Lady of Perpetual Succour pray for them.
I have loved them in life and will not forget them in death – LIZZIE.

(70)

GALLAGHER
In memory of Thomas Gallagher who died 5th February 1884.

(478)

GALLAGHER
Of your charity pray for the soul of Alice Gallagher who died 23rd March 1881 aged 63 years, and other relatives of the family who are interred here.

(743)

GALLAGHER
Here lieth the remains of Charles Gallagher who died 23rd February 1816 aged 60 years.

(909)

GAMBLE
This monument was erected by James Gamble of Drogheda to the memory of William Hoare who departed this life the 1st March 1823 aged 10 months. John Hoare died 5th May 1823 aged 9 years. Christopher Bogan died 12th April 1824 aged 27 years. Also Michael Gamble
who died 5th January 1830 aged 6 years.

(737)

GARGAN
Erected by Ann Gargan of Trinity Street in memory of her husband Edward Gargan who died 26th January 1864 aged 31 years. Also their son Patrick died young.

(88)

GARGAN
Patrick Gargan, Sundays Gate, his son Patrick died 28th August 1876 aged 16 years, and his mother-in-law Alice Woods R.I.P.

(218)

GARGAN
See Kiely.

(85)

GARLAND
Erected by Mary Garland of Hand Street in memory of her husband Thomas Garland who died 2nd August 1880 aged 60 years and their children Joseph and Thomas who died young.

(422)

GARTLAND
Erected by James Gartland of Scarlet Street in memory of his wife who died 15th October 1875 aged 65 years.

(739)

GARTLAND
Erected by Patrick Gartland of Hardmans Garden in memory of his father and mother Thomas and Mary Gartland. Also his son James who died in St. Louis, U.S.A. aged 18 years, and his daughter Margaret who died 20th May 1853 aged 4 years, and his grandchild Peter Mathews who died young, and Thomas Gartland died 27th January 1884

(887)

GARTLANY
This stone was erected by C. Gartlany in memory of her daughter Mary who died 24th December 1877. Also her husband Thomas who died 23rd December 1879.

(731)

GARVEY
1880 Erected by Henry Garvey in memory of his two children who died young.

(117)

GARVEY
Erected by Henry Garvey of Peter Street, Drogheda, in memory of his wife Elizabeth who died 18th June 1894 and two of his children who died young and the above Henry Garvey died 18th August 1894 aged 52 years.

(474)

GARVEY
Erected by John Garvey, Black Bull, in memory of his son Patrick who died 10th March 1873 aged 26 years. Also his son Owen who died 5th June 1873 aged 19 years.

(493)

GARVEY
See Murphy.

(491)

GAYNOR
Erected by James Gaynor of the Marsh in memory of his mother Elizabeth Gaynor who died 12th June 1889 aged 88 years.

(239)

GAYNOR
Mrs. Mary Gaynor of Drogheda in memory of her beloved husband Laurence Gaynor late of Sunday Gate who died 1st February 1815 aged 50 years. Also her daughter Anne who died 8th November 1828 aged 16 years. Also two of her sons Patrick and John who died young. Interred also the remains of Mrs. Anne Gahagan her sister who died 7th March 1832 aged 62 years.

(744)

GAYNOR
Erected AD 1879 by Kate Gaynor in memory of her mother Bridget Gaynor of Harmons Garden and her brother Patrick.
(892)

GERRARD
Erected by Mrs. Gerrard in memory of her husband Thomas.
(897)

GERRARD
The burial place of James Gerrard. Here lies the remains of his beloved wife Margaret Gerrard who died 9th March 1835.
(926)

GERNON
Alice Louisa Gernon 4th December 1916. Margaret Gernon 13th February 1891 aged 84. (Two coffins in the vault).

GIBBONS
Erected by Mary Anne Gibbons, William Street, Drogheda in memory of her beloved sister BESSY who departed this life the 11th March 1847 and her aunt ALICE BRENNAN on the 14th February 1862. Also her mother on the 13th March 1871 after a protracted illness borne with patience and resignation to the inexpressible grief of her only surviving daughter and husband. She was a faithful wife and a loving mother possessing the noble virtues of a true Christian having no attachment to this world, and hoping through the mercy of God to meet her Redeemer and be reunited to her five loving children where all sorrows end in the mansions of bliss.
(245)

GIBBONS
This stone and burial place belongeth to Patrick Gibbons, his brother and their posterity 1781.
(290)

GIBNEY
In memory of Michael Gibney, 42 Bredin Street, died 30th December 1947 and his wife Bridget died 12th January 1948.
(433)

GIBNEY
Erected by Mrs. Rose Gibney, Hardmans Gardens, to the memory of her husband John Gibney who died 28th November 1878, and the above Rose Gibney died 3rd December 1889.
(538)

GIBNEY
Erected by James Gibney, Australia, in memory of his parents Thomas and Mary Gibney, the former of whom died in the year 1837 and the latter on the 17th November 1879. On whose souls Sweet Jesus have mercy.
(558)

GIBNEY
See McDonnell.
(111)

GIBSON
See Courtney.
(657)

GILL
Erected to the memory of John Gill, late of Dundalk, who departed this life 17th February 1863 in the 59th year of his age.
(728)

GILMER
Erected by Bridget Gilmer of Drogheda, in memory of her husband Francis Gilmer who died 15th October 1831 aged 55 years. Her son Thomas 6th May 1832 aged 8 years. Her son Francis 19th January 1840 aged 23 years. Her son Peter 23rd February aged 25 years, and the above Bridget Gilmer who died 1st November 1846 aged 60 years.
(875)

GILSENAN
Of your charity pray for the soul of Mary Gilsenan who died 1st March 1872, also for James Gilsenan who died 28th January 1886, and for the soul of Margaret Gilsenan who died 27th March 1892.
(505)

GINNETY
See Sisters of Charity.
(1)

GOGAN
Erected by Michael Gogan, Roughgrange, in memory of his father Michael Gogan, 22nd April 1866 aged 76 years. And his mother Margaret died 16th January 1881. Also the above named Michael died 9th December 1889 aged 65 years.
(798)

GOGARTY
In memory of Eliza the beloved wife of Laurence Gogarty of Beamore, who departed this life 22nd August 1880. The above named Laurence Gogarty died 6th March 1881 aged 83 years, also his daughter Mrs. Devin who died 25th July 1886.
(18)

GOGARTY
See McDonough.
(8)

GOLDEN
See Sisters of Charity.
(1)

GORMAN
Erected by Patrick Gorman of Peter Street in memory of his children Andrew who died 6th April 1889 aged 14 years, and Patrick who died young.
(244)

GORMAN
This burial place belongeth to John Gorman and Edward Porter and their family, 1775.
(614)

GORMLEY
Sacred to the memory of John Joseph Gormley of Peter Street, Drogheda, who died on the 25th day of September 1872 aged 49 years, also their son Vincent de Paul Gormley who died on the 27th day of April 1872 in the 19th year of his age, his daughter Eliza who died 6th February 1881, his wife Kate who died 27th November 1881 and his son Val. E. who died 1st September 1884.
(349)

GRADY
Erected by James Grady of Loughboy, Drogheda, in memory of his wife Catherine Grady who died 19th March 1835 aged 54 years. Pray for the repose of the souls of Michael O'Reilly, Trinity Street, who died 18th March 1891. Also his wife Mary died 14th November 1893.
(516)

GRAHAN
See Walsh.
(812)

GREENE
Erected by Thomas and Mary Greene, North Strand, in memory of Thomas and Anne Faulkner parents of Mary Greens who died the latter on the 23 and the former on the 24th February 1855 aged respectively 76 and 73 years.
(320)

GREENE
Erected by Catherine Greene, North Strand, in memory of her husband James Greene who died 9th December 1877 aged 60 years.
(318)

GREENE
Sacred heart of Jesus have mercy on the soul of Catherine Greene, North Strand, who died 1st August 1907 aged 82 years, and her son John who died 29th July 1911 aged 57 years. Also her daughter Kate Greene who died 13th March 1938 aged 83 years.
(345)

GREENE
Pray for Alice Greene, Fair Street, her brother Patrick, her parents Peter Carroll and Kate and her Godmother Anne Finegan.
(371)

The Cord Cemetery

Entrance to the Cord in Thomas Street.

View looking East shows the Church gable. Photo J. Garry.

Monument to Rev. Thomas Burke, O.S.D. - beside the ruined gable. Photo J. Garry

The Mortuary Chapel in 1975. Photo J. Garry.

GREENE
Erected by Thomas Greene of Manimore in memory of his father and mother Peter and Alice Greene, who died – Alice 11th November 1853 aged 46 years – Peter died 17th December 1859 aged 57 years. Also 2 of his children – Charles Augustine died 7th September 1886 aged 5 years. Elizabeth Mary died 16th May 1887 aged 10 years. His son Thomas died 23rd June 1888 aged 21 years. The above Thomas Greene died 11th May 1881 aged 51 years. His son Joseph died 27th January 1893 aged 24 years.

(625)

GREHAN
Erected by Catherine Grehan, Mell, in memory of her daughter Anne Grehan who died 4th January 1862 aged 17 years. Also her son Patrick died 27th November 1865 and the above Catherine Grehan died 28th February 1866.

(828)

GRENAN
Erected AD 1809 by Richard Grenan for him and his posterity. Here lies his father and mother and five of his children. Here also lieth the above Richard Grenan who died 20th April 1816 aged 76 years and of Patt Grenan grandson of the above who died 5th August 1854 aged 40 years.

(506)

GRIMES
Erected to the memory of Michael and Mary Grimes.

(571)

GRIMES
Erected by Michael Grimes of Levins Bridge, Drogheda, to the memory of his brother Patrick Grimes who died 16th November 1869 aged 52 years, and the above Michael died 11th October 1880 aged 86 years.

(928)

GULSHEY
Sacred to the memory of Mr. Thomas Gulshey. As a testimony of esteem for his virtues and as a tribute of respect for his worth this monument has been erected by the inhabitants of Drogheda. For many years with great zeal and efficiency he discharged the office of Secretary to the Committee of this Cemetery and departed this life the 6th day of January 1841 in the 70th year of his age. May he rest in peace.

(605)

HAIKIN
Erected by Catherine Haikin in memory of her husband Thomas Haikin who died 27th May 1815 aged 56 years.

(568)

HALLARAN
Erected by Mr. William Hallaran of Drogheda in memory of his son William died 5th June 1845 aged 5 years.

(47)

HALL
Erected by James Hall in memory of his mother Elizabeth Hall.

(848)

HALL
Erected by Joseph Hall of Trinity Street, in memory of his wife Rose who died 11th July 1878 also his daughter Mary died 11th June 1888.

(956)

HALLIGAN
Erected by Patrick Halligan in memory of his son James who died 20th October 1876 in the 17th year of his age.

(224)

HALLIGAN
Erected by John Halligan of Shop Street, Drogheda, in memory of his daughters Jane died 25th July 1868 aged 16 years. Julia died young and the above John died 6th May 1896 aged 86 years.

(256)

HALLIGAN
Erected in 1840 by James Halligan of West Street, Drogheda, in memory of three of his children, John, Mary and James who died young. Also the above James Halligan who died 9th June 1849 aged 45 years and his wife Rose Mary Anne who died 31st July 1849 aged 40 years.

(604)

HALPIN
Erected by Anne Halpin, North Strand, to her husband Laurence who died 23rd February 1890. His daughter Teresa died 2nd September 1889. His mother Margaret died 5th March 1882 and his daughter Alicia died young.

(272)

HALPIN
See O'Callaghan.

(772)

HAMMOND
Beneath are interred the remains of LIZZIE the beloved wife of Arthur Hammond of Sheephouse. Born 21st December 1846. Died 17th August 1873. And of his infant son Arthur Joseph, also the remains of the above named Arthur Hammond who died 15th January 1891 aged 67 years.

(15)

HAMMOND
To the memory of Judith the beloved wife of Thomas Hammond of Sheephouse, she died 24th March 1866 in the 59th years of her age. Also Thomas Hammond who died 7th December 1871 in the 75 year of his age.

(16)

HAMILL
Erected by Henry Hamill of Drogheda in memory of his daughter Rose Anne who died 31st July 1841 aged 14 months. Here also lie interred the mortal remains of Henry Hamill who died 25th March 1842 aged 47 years.

(17)

HAMILL
Erected by Mary Hamill, Patrick Street, in memory of her husband Patrick Hamill, also their son Thomas.

(125)

HAMILL
Erected by John Hamill of Drogheda in memory of his father Patrick Hamill who died 1st January 1827 aged 70 years. Also his mother Margaret Hamill died 1st March 1856 aged 69 years. Here also lie the remains of the above John Hamill who died 23rd August 1856 aged 60 years. Also Anne wife of the above John Hamill died 21st August 1867 aged 75 years.

(734)

HAMILTON
Erected by Margaret Hamilton in memory of her mother Catherine who died 21st February 1860. Also her father John who died 3rd September 1869.

(56)

HAND
Erected by E.R. in respectful remembrance of Margaret Hand late of Duleek Street, Drogheda who died on the 23rd December 1880 aged 43 years.

(178)

HAND
Erected by Alice Hand of Drogheda in memory of her husband Michael Rody who died 29th August 1823 aged 55 years. Also Patrick and Elizabeth Corrigan and their son John 1868.

(269)

HAND
Erected by Patrick Hand of Stockwell Lane in memory of his father and mother, his infant son James Christopher and his sister-in-law Kate Clarke. Also his son Patrick who died 25th February 1921 and his wife Mary who died 1st January 1928. His daughter Rose Mary who died 1st October 1930 and the above Patrick who died 11th March 1941.

(421)

HAND
Peter Hand of Hand Street, erected this in memory of his wife Mary who died 9th May 1855 aged 40 years. The above Peter Hand died 28th November 1863 aged 57 years.

(563)

HAND
Erected by Patrick Hand of Hand Street in memory of his daughter Eliza who died infant.

(546)

HANMER
Erected by James Hanmer R.I. Constabulary Drogheda Co. In memory of his daughter Mary who resigned her youthful spirit into the hands of her Maker on the 21st March 1871 age 6 years. The above named James Hanmer died 10th March 1885 aged 60 years.

(681)

HANRATTY
Erected by Anne Hanratty of Mell as a tribute of respect to her affectionate husband Felix Hanratty who died 11th day of January 1851 aged 54 years.

(46)

HANRATTY
John Hanratty died 3rd November 1871.

(192)

HANRATTY
In memory of Laurence Hanratty, Duleek Street, who died 14th October 1883.

(855)

HARTY
Erected AD 1850 by Patrick Harty of Magdalene Street, Drogheda, to mark this humble spot for him and his posterity.

(733)

HARDMAN
This stone and burial place belongeth to Charles Hardman of Drogheda, and family, wherein lies the bodies of his father and mother. Also of his wife and four of his children 1781.

(714)

HATTON
Erected by Mr. Bernard Hatton of Shop Street, Drogheda, in memory of his beloved wife Catherine who died 24th June 1849 aged 52 years. Also five of his children who died young. His son Bernard died 8th October 1855 age 20 years. The above Mr. Bernard Hatton died 15th November 1865.

(45)

HAVERTY
Erected by John Haverty, Bredon Street, Drogheda, in memory of his wife Rose who departed this life 12th April 1872. Also in memory of her mother, four children and his posterity.

(175)

HEALY
Erected by Catherine M. Healy, West Street, in memory of her eldest son James Stanislaus Healy who departed this life 15th February 1876 aged 35 years.

Also of her youngest son Joseph R. Healy who died 21st October 1876 in the 26th year of his age. And her daughter Henrietta the beloved wife of Thomas H. Simcocks V.S. Drogheda who died 24th February 1890.

(22)

HEALY
In the Holy Name of Jesus pray for the soul of Jane the beloved wife of Luke J. Healy, West Street, who died 1st June 1889. Kathleen M. Healy died 9th November 1959.

(23)

HEALY
This stone and burial place belongeth to Patrick Healy, brouge maker, wherein lieth seven of his children. Also his wife who died 23rd November 1784 aged 49 years.

(646)

HEALY
See Fullam.

(354)

HEENEY
Erected by Julia and Mary Heeney in memory of their parents Christopher and Mary Heeney of Yellowbatter, who died the former 15th March 1877 aged 70 years, and the latter on 15th October 1876 aged 66 years.

(554)

HEENEY
Erected by Margaret Heeney, Scarlet Street, in memory of her husband Patrick who died August the thirteenth 1861.

(570)

HEENEY
Erected by James Heeney of Hand Street, in memory of his daughter Bridget who died 4th July 1849 aged 10 years. And his daughter Mary died 21st April 1856 aged 24 years. The above James Heeney died 10th November 1857 aged 60 years.

(761)

HEENEY
Erected by Patrick Heeney of Drogheda in memory of his wife Margaret Heeney, who died 14th February 1855, the above Patrick Heeney died November 1878. Also his daughter Mrs. Mary Burns who died 13th April 1884.

(930)

HEFFERNAN
In memory of Edward Heffernan who died 15th June 1876 aged 65 years.

(102)

HICKEY
This stone was erected by Jane Hickey to the memory of her beloved husband James Hickey, grocer, and late of Laurence Street, Drogheda, who died 26th February 1863 aged 39 years. Also their infant child Rose who died young. The above Jane Hickey died 19th June 1873 aged 45 years.

(609)

HICKEY
Erected AD 1813 by Thomas Hickey of Newtown Stangleban, in memory of his father Andrew Hickey who departed this life 1760 aged 64 years.

(685)

HIGGINS
Mary Higgins of America 1877.

(170)

HIGGINS
John Higgins of Drogheda erected this in memory of his mother Elenor Higgins who died 3rd September 1844 aged 72 years. Also his sister Mary Browne who died 26th July 1849 aged 47 years.

(591)

HILLIRD
Erected by Thomas Hillird, Magdalene Street, in memory of his daughter Alice who died 8th April 188 in the 19th year of her age. The above Thomas died 20th December 1902 and his wife Mary died 1st March 1906.

(471)

HOARE
See Gamble.

(737)

HOEY
See Murphy.

(727)

HOGAN
Erected by Patrick Hogan AD 1851 in memory of his wife Catherine who died 25th April 1851 aged 32 years. The above named Patrick died 25th May 1885 aged 76 years.

(95)

HOLMES
Erected by John Holmes in memory of his wife Catherine Holmes died 22nd August 1842 aged 53 years and his son James who died young.

(99)

HOLMES
To the memory of William Holmes Esq., who departed this life 13th of June 1841 aged 24 years. And also to the memory of his brother George Francis Holmes Esq., who died 25th June 1843 aged 23 years. Underneath is interred the body of Thomas Lynch Esq., Surgeon of Drogheda, brother-in-law of the above William Holmes, who died 27th August 1843 in the 33rd year of his age. Also his infant son Terence George who died 21st December 1841 aged 2 years.
(316)

HONE
Erected by Edgar Hone in memory of his daughter Julia who died 24th December 1873 aged 11 months, and Rose Anne Farrell who died 31st August 1975.
(447)

HORAN
See Carney.
(472)

HORNE
See Tallon.
(369)

HORRIS
Erected by John Horris, Trinity Street, in memory of his wife Bridget who died 18th March 1877.
(142)

HUGHES
Erected by Mrs. Catherine Hughes, 83 West Street, in memory of her beloved husband Edward Hughes who died 22nd March 1885 aged 73 years.
(19)

HUGHES
Sacred to the memory of James Hughes, Nuns Walk, who died 31st July 1914, his sister Catherine who died 10th March 1917 also their father and mother and relatives.
(429)

HUGHES
Erected by James Hughes out Johns Gate in memory of his daughter Catherine who died 16th February 1853 aged 21 years. Also the above James Hughes who died 17th April 1858 aged 72 years.
(512)

HUGHES
Erected by Bridget Hughes of Yellowbatter, in memory of her father and mother Michael and Bridget Hughes, who died the former in 1873 aged 62 years and the latter in 1874 aged 72 years.
(764)

HUGHES
Erected by James and Anne Hughes in memory of their beloved son James died 9th August 1883 aged 19 months.

(844)

HUGHES
Erected by Anne Hughes alias Kennedy, to the memory of her uncle Patrick Kelly Esq., T.C. Drogheda, who departed this life on the 25th day of May 1855 in the 68 year of his age. Also her mother Mrs. Anne Kennedy who died on 9th June 1856 aged 70 years. And her husband Mr. John Hughes, proprietor of the Drogheda Argus who died 7th October 1885 aged 65 years. Sacred Heart of Jesus have mercy on the soul of the above named Anne Hughes who died 2nd February 1904. Interred in the new cemetery.

(919)

(The last named Anne Hughes (nee Kennedy) was the "A. Hughes, Printer and Stationer, 111 West Street, Drogheda." who published at the request of the Siena Nuns – the History of Drogheda – in 1892, compiled and reprinted from the Drogheda Argus newspaper.

Anne Hughes had correspondence with John Boyle O'Reilly, when in 1888, she wrote him in Boston, seeking permission to publish his MOONDYNE JOE. See his reply in JODS. No.11. p51.

*The Local Government Board Sealed Order for closure of the Cord in 1893, was causing concern for many families, and the above is another example of separation. Anne Hughes was buried in the "new cemetery"– St. Peter's, as were her daughters, Mary McKeown, St. Joseph", Laytown. (1948) and Ada McKeown. (1951). (See **"St. Peter's Cemetery".***) J. Garry. 1993. P128.

The Argus Office at 111 West Street.

JACKSON
Erected by Bridget Jackson in memory of her parents John and Jane Jackson. Also the above Bridget Jackson died 4th November 1895.

(873)

JONES
See Keappock.
(753)

JOHNSON
Erected AD 1850 by Captain Bernard Johnson of Drogheda, in memory of his four children, Joseph, Thomas, Edward and Mary Anne who died young. Also the remains of his wife Margaret Johnson who died 3rd August 1854 age 37 years. The above Captain Johnson who died 18th January 1880 aged 69 years.
(991)

JOHNSON
1879. Erected by John Johnson of Sundays Gate, in memory of his father and mother, also his son died young. Also his wife Catherine who died 20th October 1884, his daughter Bridget who died 17th June 1885.
(109)

JOHNSON
Erected by Captain Bernard Johnson of Drogheda, in memory of his father James Johnson who died 16th February 1855 aged 70 years.
(201)

JOHNSON
Pray for the soul of Laurence Johnson of Hand Street, who died 20th September 1889 aged 85 years, and his wife Margaret who died 9th August 1890 aged 86 years.
(209)

JOHNSON
By Bernard Johnson of West Street, in memory of his son John who departed this life 28th January 1848 aged 2 years and 8 months. His wife Maryanne who died 24th July 1849 aged 75 years. Also the above Bernard died 5th December 1871 aged 62 years.
(212)

JOHNSON
Sacred to the memory of Mrs. Jane Johnson the wife of James Johnson who died 13th March 1881 aged 71 years. Their son Bernard died June 1849 aged 3 years and Nicholas 19th March 1890 aged 50 years, and the above James Johnson died 5th September 1891 aged 82 years.
(266)

JOHNSON
Erected by Margaret Johnson of Sundays Gate, in memory of her husband John who died 26th December 1892. Also their three children who died young and the above Margaret died 24th July 1916.
(367)

JOHNSON
Erected AD 1849 by Patrick Johnson of Drogheda in memory of six of his children.
(561)

JONSTONE
See Kelly.
(801)

KAIN
See Treanor.
(760)

KANE
Mary Kane died 14th May 1883.
(250)

KANE
See also Cane.
(484)

KAVANAGH
Margaret Kavanagh erected this stone in memory of her mother Maria Clinton who died 27th July 1880.
(264)

KAVANAGH
See Dowd.
(434)

KEALY
See Kelly
(193)

KEANE
Erected by John Keane Officer of Excise Drogheda in memory of his beloved wife Sarah who died on the 29th November 1834, aged 46 years. Also his daughter Charlotte who died on the 17th June 1847 in the 21st year of her life. Here also is Mrs Sarah Keane who died 20th March 1848.
The above James Keane died in Dublin on the 12th August 1864 and his second wife Mary who died in Dublin on the 7th August 1887 aged 84 years.
(752)

KEAPPOCK
Erected AD 1858 by Anthony Keappock of West St., Drogheda in memory of his wife Catherine who died on the 11th August 1843. Also his six children who died young. His daughter Jane Carr late of Liverpool who died 1st September 1855. And the above named Anthony Keappock who died 31st March 1862 and his son Anthony who died 1st May 1869.
Mrs Kate McConnell, daughter of the above died 11th February 1889. And James Jones Keappock son of the above died 2nd March 1898 and is interred in the vault of the Mortuary Chapel.
(753)

KEAPPOCK
James Keappock 2nd March 1898.
(A coffin in the vault)

KEARNS
I.H.S Owen Kearns died AD 1867.
(104)

KEARNS
See Byrne.
(766)

KEENAN
Erected by James Keenan of Hand Street in memory of his wife Anne who died 22nd December 1874 aged 67 years. The above James died on the 17th of November 1878 aged 72 years.
(66)

KEENAN
See Devin.
(589)

KEEGAN
See McDonnell.
(110)

KEELY
Erected by James Keely in memory of his sister Mary who died July 1858, Thomas Keely, 4th August 1875. Also his mother Charlotte who died 2nd November 1882.
(877)

KEIRNAN
John Keirnan of _____ to the memory of his son Thomas who died 25th January 1823 aged 25 years. Also the above named John Keirnan, 15th July 1881 aged 60 years.
(This stone is flaking badly)
(758)

KELLY
Erected by William Kelly, William Street in memory of his children Susan who died 24th May 1862 aged 6 years. Ellen died 18th August 1879 aged 15 years. Agnes died 13th July 1881 aged 15 years and Susannah died 13th October 1881 aged 13 years. Winefred died 5th May 1888 aged 12 years, and Mary Anne eldest daughter of the above Mr. Kelly who died 1st October 1895. May the Lord have mercy on their souls.
(155)

KELLY
Erected by William Kelly in memory of his daughter Marianne who died 29th April 1858 aged 19 years, late of Peter Street. Also his wife Susan who died 21st October 1873, also the above William Kelly who died 25th October 1887 aged 89 years.
(156)

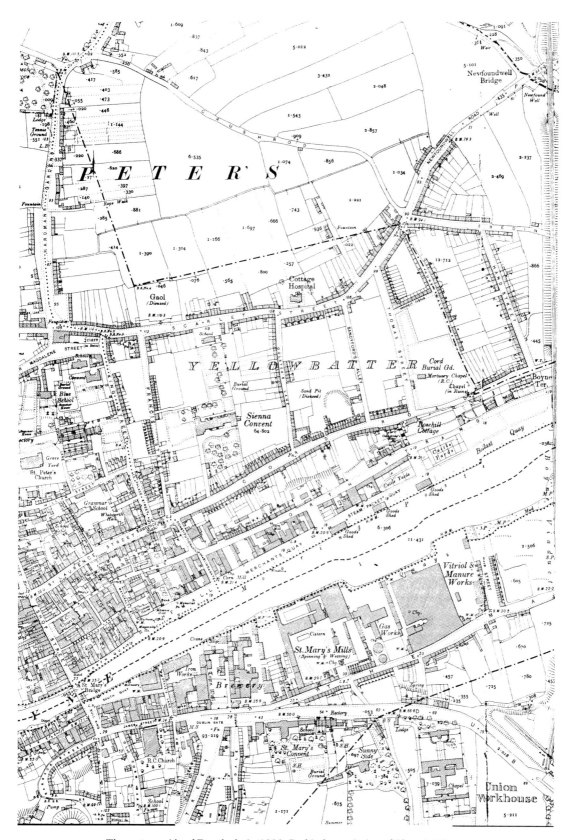

The eastern side of Drogheda in 1908. By kind permission of Phoenix Maps.

KELLY
Erected AD. 1881 by James Kelly of the Twenties, Drogheda, in memory of his father and mother and his beloved wife Mary Kelly.

(193)

KELLY
Erected by Mathew Kelly in memory of his father James Kelly. His son James Augustine Kelly, born 16th August 1873, died 12th October 1880. And the above Mathew Kelly and his brother Laurence who were lost at sea 12th December 1883 leaving a sorrowing wife and an aged mother to mourn their loss.

(257)

KELLY
Erected by the Misses Kelly, Boyne Terrace, to the memory of their sister Elizabeth who died 11th March 1854 and of their sisters Marianne and Jane the former having died on 4th July 1865 and the latter on 21st August 1865 and of their cousin Mrs. Mary Boyle who died 20th October 1871. Also their brother Mr. Bernard Kelly who died 18th December 1872. Also of Kate Kelly who died in Dublin 11th March 1888 and Alice Kelly who died at Rathmullen, 25th February 1890.

(310A)

KELLY
This stone was erected by John Kelly of Hand Street in memory of his wife Mary Kelly who departed this life 12th April 1848 aged 30 years and four of his children who died young.

(336)

KELLY
In memory of Walter Kelly T.C. Dyer Street, Drogheda who died 10th November 1884 aged 42 years. Also his daughter Jane Josephine who died 29th January 1887 aged 3 years and four months.

(365)

KELLY
In memory of Laurence Kelly, West Street who died 18th May 1888, his wife Mary Jane died 30th December 1906 and their children John Francis died 4th November 1903 and Josephine died 2nd October 1900.

(399)

KELLY
Erected by William Kelly, Magdelene Street in memory of his beloved son William J. Kelly who died 4th May 1902 aged 29 years and the above William Kelly died 1st December 1903 aged 76 years.

(417)

KELLY
In memory of William Kelly, Magdalene Street who died 4th May 1902 aged 29 years and his father William who died 1st December 1903 age 76 years. Also his mother Mary who died 25th June 1913 aged 82 years. By their daughter Jane Negrose of Montgomery A1a.

(417)

KELLY
O adorable Heart of Jesus give eternal rest to the souls of Patrick Kelly, Bull Ring who died 23rd October 1895 and Mrs. Curley who died 23rd March 1901, also his son Patrick Francis who died 28th July 1925 and his wife Mary A. who died 5th November 1931.

(427)

KELLY
Sacred Heart of Jesus have mercy on the souls of Captain Michael Kelly died 19th January 1893 aged 68 years. His wife Marianne died 27th December 1900 aged 79 years. His son John died 27th July 1903, his grandaughter Lilly McDermot died 29th November 1918. His son Thomas who was drowned at sea June 1876.
Also his son-in-law Mortimer M. Simington who was also drowned at sea November 1900. Here also are interred his three grandchildren Nora and Madeline McDermot and May Simington who died young. His grandchild Francis McDermot who died 1st February 1922. His daughter Elizabeth Simington who died 23rd December 1932.

(452)

KELLY
Alice Kelly died 12th July 1883 aged 21 yrs.

(465)

KELLY
+ Kelly

(475)

KELLY
James Kelly, Westgate, Drogheda, in memory of his wife Bridget who died 29th August 1860 aged 60 years and his son James who died 6th December 1859 aged 31 years. His daughter Mrs. Anne Finnegan died 19th June 1860 aged 40 years. His son Owen died young. The above James Kelly died 11th January 1861 aged 65 years. His daughter Mrs. Margaret Boyle who died 9th March 1883 aged 65 years.

(523)

KELLY
Erected AD 1865 by Anna Francis Kelly in memory of her father John Kelly of the North Strand, Drogheda, Master Mariner who died 12th February 1859 and her mother Susan Teresa Kelly who died 3rd June 1863.

(626)

KELLY
Erected by Peter Kelly of Cannonstown, in memory of his wife Jane Kelly who died 18th September 1872 aged 60 years.

(636)

KELLY
This Stone was erected AD 1848 by John Kelly Esq. Of West Street, Drogheda in memory of his only and dearly beloved son James aged 9 years, who died the 13th August 1847. Also his two infant children Catherine and Martha who knew them best will deepest sigh and wish like them to live and die. Also the above John Kelly died 8th September 1865 aged 52 years and his wife Mrs. Judith Kelly died 7th December 1870

(656)

KELLY
Erected AD 1799 by James Kelly of Drogheda, Callendar Man in memory of his father Patrick Kelly who died 13th May 1798 aged 56 years. Also two of his children.
(679)

KELLY
Patrick Kelly, Bullring, in memory of four of his children who died young.
(724)

KELLY
John Kelly, Duleek Street in memory of his mother Catherine who died 11th March 1860 aged 75 years.
(741)

KELLY
This stone was erected by James Kelly of Johns Gate wherein lies the body of his mother and five of his children 1781. Also his daughter Rose.
(765)

KELLY
Pray for the souls of John Kelly and children. Also his sonñinñlaw James McNally and child. Also Mary wife of the above James McNally.
(800)

KELLY
Mary Kelly of Drogheda in memory of her mother Jane Banks who died 30th January 1829 aged 52 years. Also her daughter Catherine Jonstone who died 3rd March 1836 aged 18 years and her father William Banks died 9th March 1838 aged 70 years.
(801)

KELLY
Erected by Catherine Kelly in memory of her husband Michael Kelly, a native of Tuam, County Galway, who died 7th March 1876 aged 65 years.
(838)

KELLY
Erected by Michael Kelly, Duleek Street, in memory of his daughter Catherine who died 8th April 1880.
(868)

KELLY
Erected by Eliza Kelly, Dublin Road, in memory of her brother James Kelly who died 5th February 1874.
(902)

KELLY
Erected by Patrick Kelly of Drogheda in memory of his brother John Kelly who died 4th December 1835 aged 40 years.
(920)

KELLY
Erected by Captain Patrick Kelly in memory of his beloved parents Peter and Mary Kelly who died the former 28 March 1846 and the latter 22nd May 1868. Also his brother Captain Peter Kelly who died at sea 16th August 1873. His daughter Margaret died 14th June 1884 aged 14 years and two children Mary and John who died young.

(943)

KELLY
Matthew J. Kelly, N.T. Dunleer Boys N.S. died 15th March 1943 age 37 years. Also his parents Mary & James Kelly who died 2nd February 1928 and 25th June 1936. Ar dheis De go rabh a n-anamnacha

(Matt Kelly, who died a relatively young man, was a Council member of the Co. Louth Archaeological Society, from 1939 to 1943. As one of the Drogheda Sub-Committee of that Society, he contributed learned articles of Drogheda interest to the Journal of the Society. "Two Castles of Drogheda" (1939): "St. Saviour's, Drogheda"(1940): "Bathe House and other Wooden Houses" (1941) and "Three Drogheda Monasteries" (1941).

KELLY
See Murphy.

(61)

KENNEDY
Erected by Bridget Kennedy of North Quay, Drogheda in memory of her husband James Kennedy who died 21st January 1861 aged 89 years and the above named Bridget Kennedy who died 28th June 1862 aged 72 years and their daughters, Eliza 22nd June 1874, Marian 4th April 1891, Rose 11th April 1892 and their son Richard J. who died 21st May 1894.

(61)

KENNEDY
John Kennedy in memory of his father-in-law James Short, his wife Margaret and their two children James and John Kennedy who died young.

(536)

KENNEDY
This burial place belongeth to Patrick Kennedy of Drogheda and his posterity.

(763)

KENNEDY
See Hughes.

(919)

KENT
Erected by Christopher Kent of Drogheda to the memory of his wife Mary who died 24th February 1843 age 56 years. Also his son Thomas who died 8th July 1848 age 20 years. His son Patrick died 3rd August 1864 and the above Christopher Kent died 2nd October 1864.

(638)

KELSH
Erected by James Kelsh in memory of his mother Bridget Kelsh Ogle who died 5th February 1870 in the 66th year of her age and her son George Ogle who died 1st January 1887 aged 48 years.

(195)

KERLEY
In memory of Thomas Kerley of Fair Street, Drogheda. Born 18th February 1814. Died 5th May 1881. R.I.P.

(572)

KERLEY
Erected by Margaret Kerley to the memory of her beloved husband Michael Kerley late of Fair Street, Drogheda, who died 12th November 1837 aged 69 years. Also her daughter Mrs. Murray who died 14th January 1875 aged 73 years.

(573)

KERRIGAN
Erected by Julia Kerrigan, Cord Road in memory of her husband Thomas who died 25th March 1895. Also her daughter Julia Josephine who died 25th November 1881.

(51)

KEOGH
See Rourke.

(446)

KEVITT
See McKevitt.

(411)

KIELY
Erected by Bridget Kiely in memory of her son Patrick Kiely who died 27th April 1893 and her mother Catherine Gargan who died 24th February 1888, also her brother Patrick Gargan died 26th December 1869 and his wife Bridget died March 1871.

(85)

KIERAN
Erected by William P. Kieran of Malahide in memory of his wife Agnes who died 6th February 1891 aged 38 years. Sacred heart of Jesus have mercy on her soul, and the above William Kieran who died 27th September 1927. Compassionate Lord Jesus give eternal rest to his soul. Also their son Ernest Francis who died 23rd February 1936 aged 50 years. May the Lord have mercy on his soul.

(378)

KIERANS
Pray for the soul of Anne Kierans who died 1874.

(782)

KING
Mrs. Anne King of Mell erected this stone in memory of her husband John King who died 18th May 1873 and two of their children Agnes and John who died young. Also her daughter Kate who died 20th May 1880 aged 17 years.

(588)

KING
See McKeever.
(273)

KING
See Sisters of Charity.
(841)

KINLAN
Erected by Patrick Kinlan of Hand Street in memory of his wife Catherine, 9th April 1875. Also his children Bridget and Margaret who died young.
(294)

KIRWAN
In loving memory of Captain Edward Kirwan who died 29th July 1917 and his father and mother and his sister Julia Callaghan who died 8th February 1944.
(350)

KIRWAN
Erected by John Kirwan of Drogheda in memory of his father Edward Kirwan, died 20th July 1832 aged 74 years. Also his mother Mary Kirwan died 2nd January 1825 aged 64 years. Likewise three of his brethren viz Patrick, Peter and Michael. Also his sister Anne Bisset who died 12th July 1854 aged 48 years. The above John Kirwan died 18 November 1870 aged 67 years. His son Joseph 16th March 1881 aged 26 years.
(528)

KIRWAN
Erected by Edward Kirwan Master Mariner, Drogheda, in memory of his father Henry Kirwan who died 15th December 1842. Also his sister Mary died 20th September 1868 and his mother Anne Kirwan who died 31st August 1869.
(574)

KIRWAN
See Moore.
(404)

KNOWLES
Patrick Knowles of Duleek Street, in memory of his brother John who died 17th June 1876 aged 28 years, also his mother Anne who died 19th April 1880.
(128)

LAMB
Erected by Peter Lamb of Hardmans Gardens in memory of his son Peter who departed this life 11th August 1848 aged 19 years.
(226)

LANDERS
See Levins.
(722)

LARKEN
This stone was erected by Stephen Larken where lies three of his children. Also his son John Larken who died 20th march 1774 age 9 years.

(674)

LARKIN
Sacred to the memory of Catherine the wife of Patrick Larkin Esq. who died in January 1853 aged 32 years, also her infant child.

(184)

LAWLESS
Erected by Mrs. Lawless in memory of her husband Henry Lawless who died 18th November 1846 aged 42 years and their son William who died 6th January 1861 aged 23 years.

(141)

LEE
Here lieth the body of Luke Lee who departed this life the 25th September 1778 aged 35 years.

(289)

LEECH
Erected by Captain Andrew Leech in memory of his children, Kate died March 1875 aged 13 years, Margaret died 7th February 1879 aged 19 years, Lillie and Ellie who died young.

(601)

LENNOD
Here lieth the body of Thomas Lennod who was murdered the 25th of June 1773 aged 29 years.

(487)

LEONARD
Erected by John Leonard of Thomas Street in memory of his parents John and Catherine who are interred here.

(617)

LEONARD
See McGovern.

(639)

LEVINS
George Levins, 1868.

(265)

LEVINS
In memory of Anne Levins who died 19th August 1891 aged 70 years and her sister Catherine Shiels who died 7th September 1902.

(401)

LEVINS
In memory of Catherine beloved wife of James Levins of Drogheda who died 25th August 1855. His daughter Bridget died 30th November 1857 and his sons James died 17th October 1868, Daniel died 5th December 1868 and the above James Levins who died 11th May 1879. His son Joseph died 21st November 1879. This monument was erected as an affectionate memorial by the surviving children of the above James and Catherine Levins.

(598)

LEVINS
Underneath lie the remains of Bridget, daughter of Michael Levins of Drogheda, Woollen Draper, who exchanged this world for a better on the 21st February 1823 aged 7 years. Also his son Michael who died an infant. And his son James who died on his return from Arequipa in South America in the 22nd year of his age. His daughter Marcella aged 3 years. His second wife Mary Anne Levins whose maiden name was Flyn who died in the 29th year of her age. Universally and deservelly regretted. She was a model for step-mothers, as her kindness to the children of his first wife could not be exceeded by their own mother. And his daughter Agnes who died 2nd October 1840 aged 22 years. His daughter Marianne died 10th March 1841 aged 27 years. His son John Levins died 2nd November 1843 aged 10 years. Here also lie the remains of the above Michael Levins who exchanged this temporal for eternal life on the 2nd November 1846 aged 65 years. He was for so many years a highly respectable trader in Drogheda fulfilling his duty in all relations of life as a practical Christian and an ardent Patriot.
Also his daughter Rose Levins who died 27th January 1871 aged 66 years.

(721)

LEVINS
Erected by Margaret Levins of Ropewalk in memory of her husband Patrick Levins who died 16th June 1823 aged 61 years. Also their daughter Mary Landers who died 9th August 1875 aged 75 years.

(722)

LITCHFIELD
Erected by Mary Litchfield in memory of her husband James who died 16th January 1872. May his soul rest in peace.

(936)

LONG
In memory of Captain Thomas Long who died 30th March 1856 and his wife Eliza died 22nd March 1873, also his sister-in-law Maria Dullaghan who died 27th February 1887.

(64)

LONG
Erected by Captain Thomas Long of John Street in memory of his infant son Thomas and his daughter Mary Jane and his wife Eliza who died 28th March 1883. Also his son John Joseph who died 10th October 1900 aged 25 years and the above Captain Thomas Long who died 23rd November 1913 and his son Patrick who died 21st February 1938.

(397)

LONG
Erected by Thomas Long of John Street, in affectionate remembrance of his brother Captain John Long who was lost at sea in August 1881. Of your charity pray for the soul of a beloved brother and father.

(398)

LONG
Erected AD 1st May 1843 by Patt Long of Drogheda in memory of his posterity who lie here.

(585)

LOUGHRAN
See Odair.

(140)

LOWTHE/LAWERENS
Extracts from Isaac Butler's Journal, 1744, published in CLAJ. Vol.V.(1922) has the following......At a small distance from St. Lawrence's Gate there is the remains of an old Abbey which the inhabitants call Corde or Nunn's Walk, it has been considerable and a place of great interment, as appears from the fragment of a fine tomb all destroyed, what was remaining on it as followeth;

> Hiear under lieth the corpses of Charles St. (Law)rens second brother to the Lord Baron Lowthe (recte Howthe), Margaret Elcock his wife.

+ +
CSL ME

In the same issue there are footnotes by J.R. Garstin, Esq., Bragganstown.............I have no doubt that LOWTHE is a mistake for HOWTHE. The "rens" given as the final syllable of the name is that of St. Lawrens, and to confirm this the triple initials, C.S.I. at foot indicate Charles Lawrence. In Johnson's History of Drogheda, it is said that there is in the churchyard, a monument to Lord Howth...........The St. Laurence's were long connected with the district as appears from the Inquisition – See Extract from Johnson's Drogheda, p17 suggesting that the St. Laurence Gate derived its name from them........Which Lord Howth has a brother Charles, married to Margaret Elcock??. Elcock, a Drogheda family, see tomb in St. Peter's and inscription in West Street on house built 1583 by Nicholas Elcock. (printed in Johnson's p72) To fix the date.............

Garstin draws heavily from Johnson and quotes himÖa branch of the St. Laurence family was married to a sister of Jenico (Lord) Gormanstown who was interred in the Cord burial ground. "I was unable to find the tombstone in 1910".

On page 80 Johnson has.........Here is (1826) the monumental stone belonging to the St. Laurence family, beneath which was interred the body of Richard (so) Lord of Howth. The date is not to be seen but the stone appears to be very ancient...........I regret to say it has been removed from its original place, and has thereby been broken and the inscription greatly defaced.................

In the following Journal (1923), C. MacNeill answers the question.. "There was a Charles St. Lawrence, second son of William, Lord Howth (who died 1671) and brother of Thomas, Lord Howth, 1671-1727. Elrington Ball in his "Howth and its Owners" p124, says the father left his English estates to Charles, which may explain his having a "fine Tomb", but it is rather soon in 1744 to have the tomb of a man so recently dead, "all destroyed" unless indeed it was done through political malice.

The St. Lawrences were Jacobites and Charle's brother did not apparently adhere completely to the revolution until 1697, been then 35 years old.

In Memorials of the Dead Edit by Col. P.V. Vigors. FRSAI, vol.1.1888-91 p446, the following was recorded as the "fragments left in the Cord"

LOWTHE
Hier under lieth the corpses of CHARLES..............RENS, second brother of the Lord Baron Lowthe, and Margaret Elcock.

        C-L   M-E
        _____

In 1975 the author of this list saw two broken pieces near the ruined gable which had the following in capital letters.............

    D THE 24 NOVEMBER 1613 AND WAS SONN...................

(757)

LYNAGH
Erected to the memory of Thomas Lynagh who died 16th March 1854 in his 15th year.

(263)

LYNCH
Erected by Mrs. Margaret Lynch in memory of her daughter Anne who died 25th January 1876 aged 28 years and the above Mrs. Lynch who died 21st February 1878 aged 68 years.

(208)

LYNCH
Here lieth the body of Mr. James Lynch of Drogheda. Merchant who departed this life 27th January 1783, aged 46 years. Also five of his children and his wife Mrs Ann Lynch who died 16th February 1784 aged 42 years.

(677)

LYNCH
Erected by Patrick Lynch, Old Hill, Drogheda, in memory of his son John who died 14th July 1855 aged 26 years.

(921)

LYNCH
See Holmes.

(316)

LYNES
See Byrne.

(835)

LYONS
This Stone and Burial Place belongeth to Edward Lyons where lies the bodies of three of his children 1764.

(282)

LYONS
In memory of Capt. James Lyons of Newfoundwell who died 7th November 1876 and his beloved wife Anne who died 15th January 1867. Also their infant daughter

(62)

The Cord Cemetery

JACOBITE PENNY FOUND
Yesterday week a working man, whilst engaged taking down portion of the wall of an old thatched cabin, near that ancient burial place - the Cord Cemetery, found a bronze penny, belonging to the reign of King James the Second, and dated 1689. The coin is in excellent preservation. On one side it bears the King's head with the Latin words "IACABUS II, DEI GRATIA"
On the other side is the Crown with the-letters on either side, "I.R." and around the edge the words :-"1689. MAG.BR.FRA ET HIB.REX."

Drogheda Argus, 2nd June 1894.
The above was found by Jim Garry, in the National Library, while reading there, 14th December 1989.

McARDLE
Erected by James McArdle of Old Hill, Drogheda in memory of his three children who died young. Also his son James who died 10th July 1832 aged 7 years. His wife Bridget 23rd April 1855 aged 35 years. Also his son John 30th August 1866 aged 18 years.

(94)

McARDLE
Erected by John McArdle 19 Shop Street, Drogheda, in memory of his daughter Mary Elizabeth who died 3rd September 1889 aged 2 years and 8 months. Also the above John died September 18th 1893 aged 34 years.

(386)

McAREVEY
Sacred to the memory of Bernard McArevey, Drogheda who died 28th October 1894 aged 85 years and his wife Catherine who died 23rd January 1908 aged 75 years and their sons: John died 13th February 1887 aged 32 years; William died 9th March 1888 aged 27 years; Thomas died 28th June 1907 aged 36 years.

(388)

McAULEY
Erected by John J. McAuley, Newtown, in memory of his father Peter, died 12th February 1900. Also his mother Margaret died 19th December 1923, their two daughters, Margaret and Annie, died 1st & 2nd November 1918 and their son Michael died 12th December 1953.

(357)

McCABE
Erected by John McCabe of Greenhills in memory of his two children Bridget and Margaret. Also his brother James McCabe aged 70 years. Mathew son of the above died 5th September 1886 aged 22 years.

(84)

McCABE
Sacred to the memory of Mrs. Margaret McCabe late of West Street, Drogheda who departed this life 8th December 1847 aged 72 years. Also her husband Mr. Patrick McCabe who died 18th February 1848

aged 66 years and their daughter Alicia, the beloved wife of Mr. Patrick Carr, who died 26th July 1849 aged 38 years.

(194)

McCABE
See Clarke.

(937)

McCANN
Erected by Henry McCann of Drogheda in memory of his wife Margaret McCann who died 8th January 1849 aged 60 years. His son Michael died 9th September 1849 aged 34 years.

(299)

McCANN
Anne McCann, Greenhills died 5th March 1892 and her husband Joseph 8th March 1892 aged 50 years.

McCANN
Erected by John McCann in memory of his three sons, two Johns and Patrick, who died young. Also his father Patrick McCann, 3rd October 1818 aged 67 years. His daughter Margaret died 24th May 1827 aged 7 years.

(300)

McCANN
Erected by Mary McCann in memory of her father and mother Henry and Mary Clair.

(457)

McCANN
Sacred to the memory of Carberry McCann of Drogheda who died 18th April 1854 aged 46 years. Erected by Frances his wife in fond remembrance of a most affectionate husband.

(569)

McCANN
See Toner. (709)
See Frith. (716)

McCAMLEY
Henry McCamley late of Newry. His son Henry died 16th June 1842 aged 18 years. Also his daughter Margaret who died 12th September 1845 aged 22 years.

(96)

McCARTY
Erected by Denis McCarty, Free School Lane in memory of his mother Catherine McCarty who died 2nd December 1864 aged 79 years.

(133)

McCARTY
Erected by Patrick McCarty of James Street in memory of his son Richard who died 24th July 1877 aged 25 years. Also his other son John who died 23rd September 1869 aged 9 years.

(131)

McCARRY
To the memory of Mr. James McCarry late of Greenhills who died 6th January 1831 in his 72nd year. This tomb was placed here to his memory by his son Hugh who lies beneath. Also George son of the above James McCarry who died 1st April 1881 aged 72 years.

(616)

McCLAIN
Erected by Andrew McClain of Laurence Gate, Drogheda in memory of his father James McClain who died 1st November 1828 aged 55 years. Also three of his brothers and sisters who died young. Also his grandmother Anne McClain who died 15th May 1795. Also his sister Mrs. Anne Wherly, who died 30th October 1884 aged 60 year, of the Linen Hall. This stone was erected by his sister Mrs. Catherine Reilly in 1872.

(720)

McCLOUD
Erected by Catherine McCloud in memory of her beloved husband James McCloud who died 17th May 1865 aged 46 years. Also her mother and niece. Also the above Catherine who died 26th February 1866 aged 52 years.

(80)

McCLURE
Erected by Mrs. Mary McClure, Duleek Street is memory of her son James McClure who died 11th September 1865 aged 22 years. Also Catherine McClure who died young.

(151)

McCONNON
Erected by Mathew McConnon of Fair Street, Drogheda in memory of his son Mathew who died 30th July 1869 aged 16 years and the above Mathew died 9th October 1885 aged 51 years.

(247)

McCONNON
Erected A.D.1877 by Peter McConnon of West Street, Drogheda in memory of his wife and child Mrs. Rose McConnon died 13th December 1858 in the prime of her life. She was a fond and tender mother and affectionate wife. Also Peter Christopher died 14th October 1870 age 18 years. Rose Anne 29th September 1874 aged 19 years and Bridget, Patrick and Mary Jane who died young.

(610)

McCONNON
Erected by Richard McConnon in memory of his two sons, Patrick died 20th April 1858 aged 20 years and Peter died 16th July 1861 aged--.

(705)

McCONNELL
See Keappock.

(753)

McCORMACK
Erected by Bernard McCormack, Trinity Street in memory of Bridget Steward who died 25th November 1891.

(105)

McCORMACK
Erected by Bernard McCormack, Trinity Street, Drogheda, in memory of his mother Anne McCormack who died 24th September 1879 aged 69 years also his father Thomas who died 20th February 1881 aged 77 years. Also his niece Annie Mathews who died 4th July 1892 aged 32 years and his brother-in-law Edward McMahon who died 15th October 1893 aged 65 years.

(308)

McCORMACK
Erected by Maria McCormack of West Gate, Drogheda to the memory of her husband Hugh McCormack who died 11th November 1843 aged 44 years. Here also lieth the remains of Mary Ann McCormack who died 1st March 1842 aged 6 months. Also her son Hugh who died 2nd March 1846 aged 2 years.

(328)

McCOY
See Toker.

(811)

McCULLOUGH
Erected by Rose McCullough, Trinity Street in memory of her mother Rose Whearty died 6th January 1845 and her son Thomas died young.

(114)

McCUILLIN
See Sherry.

(774)

McCULLIN
Erected A.D.1845 by John McCullin of Scarlet Street in memory of two of his children who died young.

(676)

McDANIELL
Erected by John McDaniell of Cord Street in memory of his wife Mary who died 2nd February 1885 aged 35 years. Also their daughter Mary who died young.

(715)

McDERMOT
See Kelly.

(452)

McDONNEL
Pray for the soul of Christopher McDonnell youngest son of the late Christopher McDonnell, Summerhill, Drumconrath, Co. Meath who died at Drogheda 18th July 1874 over whose remains awaiting the resurrection of the dead this monument has been placed by his beloved brother Richard

McDonnell, 52 Laurence Street as a tribute of strong affection towards him and deep respect for his memory.
Also for the souls of the above named Richard McDonnell who died at Laurence Street 24th September 1882 and his brother Patrick who died 5th January 1884.

(13)

McDONNELL
Erected by Richard McDonnell to the memory of his father and mother and his sister Bridget Gibney.

(111)

McDONNELL
Erected 1880 by Richard McDonnell to the memory of Laurence and Elizabeth Plunket and their daughter Mary Ann Keegan.

(110)

McDONNELL
Sacred to the memory of Patrick McDonnell of Newfoundwell who died 14th April 1859. Also his wife Anne McDonnell died October 1872 and their daughter Mary who died January 1860 aged 17 years. Also their son John who died young.

(161)

McDONNELL
In memory of Jane McDonnell who died 8th December 1888 also her father and mother.

(248)

McDONNELL
Susan McDonnell in memory of her husband James who died 17th December 1887.

(253)

McDONNELL
Erected by William McDonnell in memory of his mother Catherine who died 27th April 1875 aged 75 years.

(476)

McDONNELL
Erected to the memory of James and Margaret McDonnell parents of Peter and John McDonnell late of Peter Street.

(508)

McDONNELL
I.H.S. Erected by Catherine McDonnell of Drogheda in memory of her beloved husband James McDonnell who departed this life 17th July 1832 in the 54th year of his age and two of his children who died young. Also the remains of Elizabeth mother to the above James who departed this life 16th January 1828 in the 83rd year of her age. Also his father Hugh who died 24th February 1829 in the 76th year of his age.

EPITAPH OF JAMES McDONNELL
WRITTEN BY HIS DAUGHTER ELIZA.

J oin me in grief all yon that do pass by
A nd view the spot where my dear father lies
M ost cruel death, that surely conquers all
E xtinguished life, and caused his sad downfall.
S weet tender sire, alas! Alas! Your fled
M ortality has ranked you with the dead.
C old, cold's the bed wherein you now do sleep
D amp, damps your couch, which often makes me weep
O ne kind reflection yields me great content
N o one that knew you but does not lament
N more you'll wipe the tear from sorrows eye
E xtend you gift or stop the orphans cry
L ow here your frame lies buried in the mould
L ord Jesus Christ have mercy on you soul.

Amen.

Also the remains of Hugh son of the above James McDonnell who died 14th January 1846 aged 27 years and his daughter Mary died 3rd July aged 23 years and the above Catherine McDonnell who died 7th July 1849 aged 56 years.

(545)

McDONNELL
Here lieth the body of Mary McDonnell who died 3rd of May 1758 aged 68 years. This stone was erected for her family.

(586)

McDONNELL
James McDonnell, Marsh who died 2nd March, 1877.

(683)

McDONNELL
Erected A.D.1824 by Mrs. Mary McDonnell in memory of her husband James McDonnell who died 16th October 1823 aged 70 years. Also her father and mother James and Bridget Reilly and Catherine her sister. Also her grand-daughter Mary Anne McKeever aged 10 years. Nicholas McKeever died 3rd December 1826 aged 40 years. Mary McDonnell died 23rd December 1826. Catherine McKeever died 1st February 1867 aged 80 years. Michael McKeever died 30th March 1877 aged 56 years.

(770)

McDONNELL
Erected in memory of Catherine McDonnell of Stameen died 10th June 1888.

(843)

McDONNELL
Sacred to the memory of Ellen the beloved wife of Andrew McDonnell of Drogheda. She died 11th August 1832 aged 20 years.

(872)

McDONNELL
See Carrolan.

(710)

McDONNELL
See McNally.

(829)

McDONOGH
In memory of Ellen the beloved wife of Michael McDonogh of Palace Street who died 22nd April 1881 aged 39 years.

(10)

McDONOUGH
Sacred to the memory of Clara Magdalen McDonough who died 21st August 1861. Also of Mr. John McDonough who died 17th March 1865 and of their Aunt Catherine Gogarty who died 13th January 1880.

(8)

McDONOUGH
Erected by James McDonough, Hand Street in memory of his father and mother also three children.

(944)

McDONOUGH
"Of your charity pray for the soul of Mary McDonough relict of the late Mathew McDonough of Drogheda who died 6th February 1877 aged 83 years. Louise wife of Edward McDonough who died 5th March 1908 and of Edward McDonough who died 19th February 1917. May they Rest in Peace."

(In September, 1973 a marble plaque bearing the above inscription was moved down to the church vaults - for safe keeping, during alterations to the building to suit Red Cross purposes.)

McDONOUGH
Louise McDonough 5th March 1908.
Edward McDonough 19th February 1917.
(Two coffins in the vault).

McENTEGART
Sacred to the memory of Mr. Edward McEntegart late of Fair Street who died 18th June 1829 aged 44 years. Also his wife Anne who died 16th June 1835 aged 38 years. Their grandson Joseph McEntegart died 2nd December 1847 in his 18th year. Mary McEntegart wife of Owen McEntegart died 11th April 1875 in the 39th year of her age. And the above Owen died 28th March 1876 age 48. His eldest daughter Mary died April 29th 1880 aged 18 years.

(576)

McENTEGART
See Thornton.

(648)

McEVOY
Erected by Thomas McEvoy of Scarlet Street, Drogheda in memory of his sons Thomas Joseph who died 21st March 1874 aged 22 and John who died 10th August 1876 aged 21. His wife Mary who died 21st October 1876 age 50. His daughter Mary who died 31st August 1877 aged 17 and the above Thomas who died 3rd March 1896 aged 75. His son James who died 9th February 1897 aged 46 and his wife Bridget 4th July 1913 aged 79 years, her son Thomas died 7th November 1946 and his wife Julia died 5th July 1947.

(353)

McEVOY
Erected by Patrick McEvoy of Windmill Lane in memory of his children Patrick Francis died 30th June 1880 aged 6 years and Mary Jane died 24th April 1887 aged 19 years, and the above Patrick McEvoy died 3rd March 1897 aged 56 years and his wife Mary Anne died 5th November 1898 aged 56 years, and his son Thomas who died 5th December 1900 aged 29 years.

(374)

McEVOY
Sacred Heart of Jesus give eternal rest to the soul of Patrick Joseph, son of John McEvoy, Patrick Street, Drogheda, who died 7th May 1892 aged 30 years and his wife Anne who died 20th December 1896 aged 64 years and the above John McEvoy died 15th October 1912 aged 78 years. Also his son John died 31st July 1914 aged 46 years and his grand daughter Anna Mary died 17th July 1918 aged 21 years and grand son Staff Lieut. Jack McEvoy who died 25th October 1922 aged 22 years.

(380)

McEVOY
Erected by Christopher McEvoy, Duleek Street in memory of his father John McEvoy who died 11th June 1889. The above Christopher died 17th September 1924.

(470)

McEVOY
Erected to the memory of Elizabeth McEvoy of 3 Cord Road who died 14th January 1874. Also Thomas McEvoy died 10th October 1878.

(824)

McEVOY
Erected to the memory of John McEvoy of James Street, Drogheda died 5th March 1852 aged 18 years.

(903)

McEVOY
See Plunket.

(557)

McGEE
Erected by John McGee of Braden Street, Drogheda in memory of five of his children.

(431)

McGEE
Erected by John McGee, Newfoundwell in memory of his wife Anne who died 5th July 1896 aged 50 years and the above John died 2nd August 1907 aged 61 years.

(431)

McGEOGH
Erected to the memory of Anne McGeogh who died 6th August 1834 aged 55 years. Also her daughter Catherine McGeogh who died 20th august 1834 aged 23 years.

(502)

McGEOUGH
In memory of Ellen McGeough who died 24th September 1878 aged 7 years.

(808)

McGEOWAN
Erected by James McGeowan of Trinity Street, Drogheda in memory of his wife Mary who died 6th March 1886 aged 47 years. Also two of her children who died young and their son Michael who died in America 19th December 1887 aged 24 years.

(883)

McGEOWN
To the memory of George McGeown who departed this life 26th September 1866 aged 23 years.

(888)

McGILL
Of your charity pray for the soul of William McGill, Cord Road who died 18th May 1890 aged 62 years.

(12)

McGLADE
Erected by Mary McGlade, Nuns Walk in memory of her son Patrick McGlade who died 21st February 1874 aged 15 years. Here also lies the remains of her father Joseph Carr and her mother Mary Carr who died 22nd March 1878 and her sister Ann Carr who died 24th October 1878.

(150)

McGOUGH
In fond and loving memory of James McGough, Fair Street, Drogheda. Fleet Engineer R.N. died 27th February 1892 aged 54 years and his mother Bridget died March 28th 1895 aged 75 years and his father Patrick died 23rd June 1895.

(358)

McGOUGH
This stone and burial place belongeth to Patrick McGough of Drogheda wherein lieth his wife Catherine McGough alias Devine who departed this life the 9th of April 1784 aged 50 years. Also three of his children.

(806)

McGOVERN
This stone was erected by Michael McGovern, North Strand in memory of his son James who departed this life 10th August 1831 aged 21 years. Also James Leonard grandfather of the said James McGovern. Also the above Michael McGovern died 12th June 1837 aged 58 years. Also his wife Margaret who died 16th June 1841 aged 72 years.

(639)

McGOVERN
Erected by Catherine McGovern of Trinity Street, in memory of her husband Patrick McGovern who departed this life 12th January 1873 aged 58 years. Also four of his children who died young.

(704)

McGRATH
Erected by Mary McGrath, Newtown, Stameen in memory of her father Patrick who died 29th May 1922, her mother Rose Anne died 10th November 1920, her brother John died 9th April 1889 and Thomas who died 1st November 1907. Her sisters, Elizabeth who died 11th February 1954 and Roseann died 27th December 1955. The above Mary died 9th July 1956 and her brother Patrick died 17th April 1957.

(402)

McGRATH
Erected by Mrs. Elizabeth McGrath, North Quay, Drogheda, in memory of her husband Thomas who died 7th June 1861 in the 37th year of his age.

(548)

McGUINNESS
Erected by John McGuinness of Patrick Street in memory of his mother Annie who died 1st April 1869 aged 78 years. Also her son Edward died 7th November 1871 aged 7 years and Patrick who died 12th July 1876 aged 14 years and the above John McGuinness who died 19th June 1889 and his wife Mary who died 17th July 1900.

(416)

McGUIRE
Pray for the soul of Margaret McGuire who died 7th September 1881 aged 75 years.

(659)

McGUIRK
Erected by Bridget McGuirk, Trinity Street in memory of her husband James who died 22nd January 1876. Also her daughter Mary died 24th November 1868.

(916)

McHUGH
Erected by Patrick McHugh, Dyer Street, in memory of his son John, 2nd March 1871.

(889)

McKANNA
This burial place belongeth to Patrick McKanna where lies two of his children 1773.

(513)

McKEEVER
Erected by Patrick McKeever, Greenhills in memory of his mother Judith McKeever who died 20th March 1867. Also his father Patrick who died January 4th 1880 and three of his brothers who died young.

(138)

The Drogheda Independent

AND
MEATH, LOUTH, MONAGHAN & CAVAN LEAGUER.
"Faith and Fatherland."

[ESTABLISHED 1884.]

Offices—7 SHOP STREET, DROGHEDA.

PRICE TWO-PENCE.

Annual Subscription—Unstamped, delivered in Town, 9/-; Half-yearly, 4/6; Quarterly, 2/3. Post Paid, 11/- per Year; Half-yearly, 5/6; Quarterly, 2/9.

THE INDEPENDENT strenuously and fearlessly maintains the great principles of Irish Nationality, and gives a zealous support to every movement having for its object the Moral, Political, and Social advancement of the People.

It is a thoroughly Catholic and National Organ.

The Paper is owned by a Company, under the name of the "Drogheda Independent" Company, Limited.

ADVERTISING.
Special Terms for Quarterly, Half-yearly, and Yearly Advertisements.

JOB PRINTING.
The facilities for turning out First-Rate Work in this Department are unexcelled.

Cheques and Post Office Orders to be made payable to the Manager.

Drogheda Independent advertisement - Bassett's Louth 1886.

Jane McQuillan

Jane McQuillan died during the L.G.B. Sealed Order for closure of the Cord in April 1893 and her burial there must have been causing concern for the family. Mrs. McQuillan, who died at her residence, 90 West Street, aged 45 years, was a tireless worker for the new church of St. Peters West Street. She is also listed on the McQuillan stone in the "new cemetery".
Courtesy. Noel McQuillan

McKEEVER
Erected by Mrs. McKeever, Drogheda in memory of her mother Mrs. Alicia relict of Christopher King of Donore. She died 7th May 1854. Also her brother-in-law Peter Mathews, Mariner who died 3rd July 1842. Also her well beloved niece Maria Mathews who died 5th August 1866.
(273)

McKEEVER
See McDonnell.
(770)

McKENNA
Erected to the memory of Thomas McKenna, North Road, Drogheda ,who died 26th November 1882. He was a respected member of every public board in Drogheda. May the Lord have mercy on his soul.
(207A)

McKENNA
Erected by Catherine McKenna, her father Thomas McKenna died 10th April 1882 aged 82 years.
(213)

McKENNA
Erected by Margaret McKenna, North Road in memory of her husband John, also their son Patrick the latter died 10th December 1856 aged 2 years the former the 25th November 1861 aged 64 years.
(296)

McKENNA
This monument was erected by his affectionate wife to the memory of Charles McKenna for many --- ---------- --lous promoter of the Cha---ies to ---- eating the female poor of Drogheda. He closed his v----- life on the 11th day of February ------- the 65th year of his age.
(Stone is badly worn.)
(305)

McKENNA
Of your Charity pray for the soul of Patrick McKenna, North Road, Drogheda who died 9th June 1890. His brother John died 8th May 1893 and his sister Catherine who died 13th February 1895. Eternal rest grant unto them O Lord.
(361)

McKENNA
Erected by Patrick McKenna of Hand Street in memory of his wife Margaret who died 6th August 1869 aged 63 years. Also his daughter Mary who died young and also his father and mother.
(552)

McKENNA
Here lies Patrick McKenna of Drogheda who died 1st March 1839 aged 34 years. And his mother Anne McKenna who died 18th November 1867 aged 86 years.
(361)

McKENNA
Erected by Mary Ann McKenna, Shop Street in memory of her husband James McKenna died 8th April 1881 aged 71 years.
(632)

McKENNA
Erected by Bridget McKenna in memory of her husband John McKenna late of Patrickswell Lane, Drogheda who died 18th January 1843 aged 71 years.

(776)

McKENNA
Erected by Catherine McKenna in memory of her husband Michael Smyth died 1827. Also her daughter Mary died 1833 and her mother Honora White died 1859 and her son John died September 1865 and the above Catherine McKenna died January 1868. Deeply lamented by her sorrowing children.

(792)

McKENNA
See Nugent.

(355)

McKENNA
See Dunleavy.

(360)

McKENNA
See Read.

(633)

McKEON
Erected by Owen McKeon in memory of his father James McKeon who died 21st January 1894 at his residence, West Gate.

(532)

McKEVITT
Erected to the memory of John and Mary McKevitt, Boher Glas who died – the former – 22nd January 1868 and the latter 18th August 1888. Also in memory of John Kevitt, Greenbatter who died 17th May 1907 and his wife Mary died 9th July 1935.

(411)

McKEW
Erected by William McKew, Winemell Lane in memory of his son and daughter James and Anne.

(90)

McKOWNE
This stone was erected in September 1777 by Thomas McKowne of Drogheda. Here lieth three of his children, his father and mother Edward & Mary McKowne. Here lieth the body of the above Thomas McKowne who departed this life 12th August 1783 aged 54 years. Mary Anne Wisdom died the 25th March 1830 aged 56 years.

(822)

McLESTER
Here lieth the remains of Edward McLester late Collector of the Port of Drogheda who died 11th June 1845 in the 58th year of his age. He was a kind friend and an affectionate husband. May he rest in peace. This stone was erected to his memory by his disconsolate widow.

(303)

McLOUGHLIN
Erected by Elizabeth McLoughlin in memory of her husband Charles who died 20th January 1825 aged 70 years.

(280)

McLOUGHLIN
Erected by Rose McLoughlin of Beltichbourne in memory of her husband Thomas McLoughlin who died 1st October 1887 aged 41 years a native of Drumconrath, Co. Meath. Their daughter Mary died November 1892 aged 14 years and the above Rose who died 3rd September 1910 aged 76 years.

(390)

McLOUGHLIN
Erected by James McLoughlin of Scarlet Street in memory of his wife Mary who died 2nd July 1853 aged 45 years. Also six children who died young. His father Michael McLoughlin died 20th November 1835 aged 60 years. His mother Bridget died 15th June 1835 aged 58 years. And the above James McLoughlin died 16th February 1872.

(762)

McMAHON
See McCormack.

(308)

McMANUS
See Flood.

(243)

McNALLY
In memory of Bridget McNally who died 5th October 1888 aged 85 years. Erected by Elizabeth McNally of Marsh Road.

(293)

McNALLY
Erected by Bernard McNally, Barnathin in memory of his father Bernard McNally died 18th February 1853 aged 46 years. Also his mother Anne McNally who died 25th November 1869 aged 66 years. His brother John McNally died 20th May 1880 aged 33 years and his uncle Patrick McDonnell died 12th January 1889 aged 92 years.

(829)

McNALLY
See Kelly.

(800)

McPHILIPS
--------- year. Also -----es McPhilips, Dyer Street.

(845)

McQUAIL
AD.1799. Erected by Hugh McQuail in memory of his mother Margaret McQuail who died 16th April 1785. Also his son Edward died April the 8th 1795 aged 17 years. Likewise his daughter Margaret McQuail who died April 14th 1797 aged 21 years.

(641)

McQUILLIAN
Erected by Peter McQuillian, West Street in memory of his father James McQuillian who died 26th January 1848 and his mother Mary died 5th March 1848. Also his daughter Anna Maria died 5th August 1883 aged 9 years and his son Patrick Joseph who died 17th March 1889 aged 19 years and his wife Jane died 26th April 1893 aged 45 years.

(65)

McQUILLIAN
Erected by Rose McQuillian in memory of her husband James McQuillian late of Hardmens Garden who died 2nd August 1845 aged 62 years.

(103)

McQUILLEN
Erected by Peter McQuillen, Green Lane, Drogheda in memory of his wife Catherine who died 17th April 1887 aged 50 years. Also the above Peter who died 8th May 1888 aged 60 years.

(420)

McQUILLAN
Michael McQuillan, Greenbatter.

(914)

MACKEN
Erected by Mrs. Maria Macken, West Street, in memory of her husband Patrick Macken who departed this life 26th July 1376 aged 49 years. Also his mother died the 15th August 1846 aged 67 years and his father who died the 4th November 1854, aged 80 years.

(833)

MACKIN
Erected by James Mackin of Drogheda in memory of his daughter Margaret who died 13th October 1831 aged 20 years. Also his son James who died 25th May 1832 aged 17 years. His wife Anne Mackin died 31st December 1836 aged 56 years.

(606)

MACKIN
See Cavanagh.

(423)

MADDEN
Erected by Daniel Madden, Greenlanes in memory of his father Henry Madden who died 21st November 1858 aged 60 years. Also his mother Esther Madden who died 20th September 1879 aged 76 years. His brother Peter Madden died 20th December 1847 aged 19 years. His sister Bridget died 2nd December 1877 age 36 years.

(672

MAGEE
Erected by Thomas Magee to his wife Margaret who died 24th December 1854 aged 66 years and the above Thomas died 15th June 1861 aged 84 years. Renewed by their grandson Thomas Byrne.
(286)

MAGEE
AD.1824. Erected By Denis Magee of Drogheda in memory of two of his sons Denis and Daniel who died as infants. Also his second son Denis and his daughter Eliza died infants.
And the above Denis Magee who died 7th June 1829 aged 40 years. His wife Bridget Anne died 6th March 1847 aged 47 years. This Stone renewed by their son Silvester D in January 1861
(842)

MAGENNIS
In memory of the Rev. Peter Magennis.
A man of pure Pieity and Sincereity of Heart.
He died in the year 1818 aged 59 years.
(755)

MAGILL
Erected to the memory of Peter Magill who died in April 1864.
(918)

MAGILL
Henry Magill, 30th December 1899, aged 60 years.
Mrs. Catherine Magill
13th March 1900, aged 87 years.
(Two coffins in the vault.)

MAGILL
See Flemin.
(787)

MAGINIS
This Stone was erected by Philip Maginis of Drogheda. Merchant in memory of his father Richard who departed this life 16th December 1772 aged 71 years and his mother Mary 28th November 1785 aged 69 years. Where also lieth interred three of the above Philip Maginis's children.
(805)

MAGINN
Erected by Christopher Maginn in memory of his father John of Cherrymount who died 1880 His mother Eliza died 1890 and his niece Bridget Byrne died 1886.
(274)

MAGINN
Erected by Julia Maginn in memory of her husband John Maginn, Chord Road, Drogheda who died 27th March 1875 aged 55 years. Also their children Lizzie and Sylvester who died young.
(931)

MAGRANE
Erected by Richard Magrane of Mell in memory of his father and mother Richard and Bridget Magrane, both of whom died on Good Friday, 23rd March 1883 aged respectively 33 and 68 years.

Also of his Aunt and Uncle Elizabeth Pentony who died 21st September 1871

Patrick Pentony died 25th January 1877 and his cousins Patrick Pentony who died 1st November 1862 and Richard Pentony died 6th October 1870.

(101)

MAGRANE
Erected by Owen Magrane Bredin St., in memory of his mother Mary who died 10th January 1889 aged 70 years and his sister Catherine who died 12th August 1890 aged 40 years. And the above Owen who died 15th April 1910 aged 73 years. Also his wife Mary (Kellys Lane) who died 28th March 1907 aged 51 years.

(335)

MAGRANE
Erected by Alice Magrane in memory of her husband Owen Magrane of Trinity St., who died 15th December 1875 aged 77 years.

(910)

MAGUIRE
Erected by Mathew Magrane in memory of his wife Anne who died 1st May 1880 aged 46 years. The above Mathew Magrane, died 10th November 1884 aged 60 years. His son Mathew died 5th September 1886 aged 22 years.

(267)

MAGUIRE
In memory of Margaret Maguire who departed from this life on the 27th of July 1871 also her father Thomas Maguire who died 4th of January 1872 and her mother Rose Maguire who died 2nd June, 1896.

(481)

MAGUIRE
Erected AD 1865 by Peter Maguire of Greenhills in memory of his son Patrick who died 18th April 1863 in the 24th year of his age....................
The above Peter Maguire died 22nd February 1883 aged 70 years.

(499)

MAGUIRE
Erected by Patrick Maguire of Drogheda. Taylor.
In memory of his wife Margaret who died March 1803.

(584)

MAGUIRE
Erected AD 1821 by Patrick Maguire of Drogheda in memory of his mother Mary Maguire who died 16th December 1816 aged 75 years

(945)

MALLON
In memory of Rose beloved wife of John Mallon, Greenlanes, who died 7th December 1894 and three of her children who died young.

(886)

MALLON
Erected by Matthew Mallen in memory of his wife Bridget who died 17th August 1883.

(947)

MALONN
H Malonn, R.I.P.

(31)

MANGAN
Erected by John Mangan, Dublin Gate, Drogheda, in memory of his son Thomas Mangan who died 19th July 1887 aged 32 years. Also the above named John Mangan who died 2nd December 1901.

(361a)

(John Mangan was a leading nationalist figure in the town during the late 1880s. He also held the unique distinction of being the only Alderman in the history of the Borough to be elected Mayor, whilst been held prisoner in Dundalk Jail, as a political suspect. On the 3rd January 1882, he was sworn in as Mayor, in the prison, and served as such for the following three months, until his release from detention.)
Source: "Return to the Bullring" Michael McEvoy.

MARGARET
One -word inscribed on a rough stone. May belong to the adjacent COFFEY plot, No 167.

(166)

MARKEY
Erected by Thomas Markey of Blackbull in memory of his wife Ellen who died 15th February 1887 and his grandchildren Ellen, Thomas, Patrick and Mary Markey.

(235)

MARKEY
Erected by Catherine Markey, Cord Road in memory of her husband Peter Mackey who died 22nd January 1899 and the above Catherine who died 30th January 1940 aged 82 years.

(394)

MARKEY
Pray for the repose of the soul of John Markey, Barrack St. Drogheda who died 14th March 1929.
His son John died 8th June 1915.
Ellen Meade died 16th September 1920.
Julia Sullivan died 2nd June 1932.

(445)

MARKEY
Erected by James Markey, Duleek Street in memory of his son Patrick who died 1st June 1873 aged 25 years. The above James Markey died 12th August 1879 aged 67 years.

(630)

MARTIN
Erected by Barthel Martin in memory of his sons and daughter Barthel, Edward and Lucy. Also his wife Rose Martin.

(86)

MARTIN
Nicholas Martin died 15th August 1877.

(136)

MARTIN
Erected by Thomas Martin, West St, Drogheda, in memory of his brother Patrick who died 31st December 1875. Also his wife Kate who died 8th September 1832 and their only child Mary Margaret who died 8th February 1883. The above Thomas Martin died 7th November 1886.

(403)

MARTIN
Erected by Thomas Martin in memory of his father Peter Martin of West Gate who died on the 4th of May 1833 aged 57 years. Also his mother Rose Martin who died 2nd February 1850 aged 70. Here also is interred John Smith of Magdalene St. who died 11th April 1384 aged 84 years and Alice Smith his wife who died 2nd September 1886 aged 75.

(509)

MARTIN
Peter Martin of Beaulieu, erected this in memory of his wife Mrs. Judith Martin who died 21st December 1845 aged 45 years. Also his son Peter who died 24th December 1867 aged 37 years. And the above Peter Martin died 1st September 1872 aged 78 years.

(599)

MARTIN
See Shiels.

(347)

MARTIN
See Fullam.

(354)

MASKELL
Mary Maskell died 16th February 1872 aged 17 years.

(288)

MASTERSON
Erected to the memory of Patrick Masterson of Shop Street who died 15th October 1871 aged 45.

(217)

MATHEWS
Erected by James Mathews of Hardmans Garden in memory of his mother Bridget Mathews who died 25th January 1885 aged 86 years.
(135)

MATHEWS
1879 Erected by Peter Mathews, Philipstown, in memory of his son John who died young………
The above named Peter Mathews died 30th April 1896. Also his wife Bridget who died 10th June 1891 and his son Thomas died 21st September 1893
(143)

MATHEWS
To the memory of Margaret M. Mathews, the infant daughter of Mr. James Mathews of Drogheda. She died 7th November 1827 aged 3 years.
(207)

MATHEWS
In memory of Michael Mathews, Kellys Lane, who died 26th September 1893 and his wife Mary died 20th December 1904 also their three daughters.
(448)

MATHEWS
Erected by Mathew Mathews in memory of his daughter Catherine who died 8th April 1881 age 40 years.
(624)

MATHEWS
Erected by Bernard Mathews of Drogheda in 1818 in memory of his daughter Catherine who died 11th October 1818 aged 7 years.
(803)

MATHEWS
In memory of George Mathews the husband of Bridget Mathews who died 5th April 1830 aged 50 years. And their daughter Bridget who died 23rd November 1864 aged 14 months. Also their daughter Bridget who died 1st July 1893 aged 15 years.
(857)

MATHEWS
See McKeever.
(273)

MATHEWS
See Faulkner.
(284)

MATHEWS
See McCormack.
(308)

MATHEWS
See Gartland.

(887)

MATTHEWS
To the memory of ANNE MATTHEWS formerly of Newtown, Drogheda, who for the long period of thirty three successive years was the faithful and confidential domestic servant of MR. WILLIAM CLINTON of Dyer Street Drogheda in whose employment she departed this life on the 26th day of December 1847 aged 60 years.

(229)

MATTERSON
Erected by James Matterson in 1807 to the memory of three of his children William, Margaret and James.

(749)

MAXWELL
Erected by Mary Maxwell in memory of her father Andrew Maxwell who died 15th May 1866 and her mother Margaret who died 23rd October 1866.

(242)

MAYPOWDER
Erected by Thomas Maypowder of Drogheda in memory of his sister Bridget Maypowder who departed this life 19th January 1841 aged 32 years and his father Thomas Maypowder who died 28th March 1841 aged 72 years.

(181)

MEADE
See Markey.

(445)

MEADITH
Erected to the memory of Wm Meadith of Drogheda and also to the memory of his son John both of whom died of cholera in October 1849. Also Anne relict of the above who died 1867.

(759)

MEDLEY
Erected AD. 1865 by Patrick Medley, Trinity St., Drogheda, in memory of his wife Bridget Medley who died 29th September 1864 aged 27 years. Also three of his children who died young.

(680)

MEEHAN
Erected by Constable Meehan of the Drogheda Constabulary in memory of his wife Maria Meehan who died 17th May 1867 aged 27 years.

(93)

MEEHAN
Erected by Julah Meehan in memory of her father and mother Patrick and Margaret Caffrey.
(495)

MEEHAN
Erected by Eliza Meehan, Duleek St., in memory of her husband John Meehan who died 26th December 1889 aged 33 years. Also her two children William and Eliza who died young.
(539)

MEEKEN
Erected by Patrick Meeken, Johns Gate, in memory of his wife Elizabeth who died 30th June 1862 aged 60 years. And his daughter Mary Anne died 1st May 1855 aged 15 years.
(189)

MEIGHAN
Erected 1850 by John Meighan. Carpenter. In memory of his wife Ann who died 4th August 1849 Also of his children who died young.
(152)

MILLER
I.H.S. Sacred to the memory of Mr. Alexander Miller who departed this life on the 7th of May 1846 aged 69 years. Here also lieth the remains of Bridget. Relict of the above Alexander Miller Also died 9th April 1855 aged 76 years. Also Christina, daughter of the above who died 29th December 1857. Also Malachi Fallon M.D., son-in-law of the above died 19th October 1866 aged 66 years. Erected by the Misses Miller.
(315)

MOHAN
Erected by Mrs. C Mohan, Bull Ring, Drogheda, in memory of her daughter Mrs. Anne Nolan who died 11th December 1869.
(832)

MOLLOY
Erected by Laurence Molloy of North Road, in memory of his wife Margaret who died 21st March 1834 aged 28 years. Also his infant child Bridget and the above Laurence Molloy died 20th June 1837 aged 32 years.
(621)

MOLLOY
Sacred to the memory of Thomas Molloy who died 2nd February 1848. Also his wife Martha who died 20th February 1849. Also four of their children who died young. Erected by their surviving children in remembrance of their many virtues.
(781)

MONAHAN
Erected by Mrs. Monahan, Cord Road in memory of her children Patrick and Laurence, the former of whom died on the 3rd and the latter on 13th of April 1877 aged respectively 14 and 22 years.
(158)

MONAGHAN
This Stone was erected by James Monaghan where lie two of his children 1775.

(498)

MOONAN
Erected by Mathew Moonan Scarlet Street Drogheda in memory of his wife Anne who died 24th March 1864. Also two of his children who died young and the above Mathew died 20th April 1874.

(241)

MOONAN
Sacred Heart of Jesus have mercy on the soul of Mary Anne Moonan who died 26th October 1917, her daughter Margaret died 7th December 1953, her son James died 15th September 1956.

(459)

MOONAN
Erected by Mrs Mary Moonan, Trinity Street, Drogheda, in memory of her husband Mr. Thomas Moonan who departed this life on the 4th day of March 1859 in the 42nd year of his age. The above Mrs. Moonan died 9th day of February 1885 aged 58 years.

(884)

MOONAN
This Cross was erected in 1886 by John Moonan, Mell Drogheda, to the memories of his father Laurence Moonan who died 26th December 1855 aged 70 years. His mother Mary Moonan died 27th October1883. His brother William Moonan also reposing underneath who died at Liverpool 13th January 1885 aged 64 years and two sisters who died young.

(885)

MOONEY
Erected by James Mooney of Hand St in memory of her daughter Margaret who died 29th July 1886 aged 8 years.

(210)

MOONEY
Erected by Christopher Mooney of Drogheda in memory of his daughter Margaret who died 16th February 1866 aged 22 years. Also one daughter who died young.

(594)

MOONEY
See Campbell.

(7)

MOORE
Erected by Laurence Moore of Drogheda in memory of his children John and Francis.

(2)

MOORE
Erected by Mr. William Moore of Cord Road in memory of his son Francis who died 14th February 1867. Also his daughter Eliza who died 10th March 1867. And the above William Moore who died 29th of October 1870 and Mary his wife who died 7th December 1835. Also his daughter Kate who died 22nd May 1892.
(42)

MOORE
Erected by John Moore of Carranstown in memory of his wife Mary Ann who died 1st August 1882 and four of their infant children. Also the above named John who died 2nd May 1911 aged 90 years. Also his daughter-in-law Rose Anne Moore, who died 30th November 7th 1929 and her son John died 7th May 1929. Also the son of the above John Moore, Thomas died 17th March 1954.
(342)

MOORE
In loving memory of Marianne Moore, Cord Road who died 16th October 1910 and her sister Winifred who died 31st October 1933 and Mary Kirwan who died 15th May 1939.
(404)

MOORE
See Boland.
(331)

MOORE
See Waliron.
(566)

MOORE
See Connor.
(858)

MORAN
Erected by Edward Moran of Drogheda in memory of his wife Mary Jane who died 7th September 1843 aged 25 years. Also his son Joseph who died young. And his daughter Mary died 21st March 1846 aged 4 years and 6 months.
(611)

MORAN
Pray for the soul of John Markey who died 10th February 1871 aged 64 years. And his wife Mary who died 14th January 1875 aged 68 years. Erected by their daughter Ellen Quinn.
(629)

MORAN
Erected by Rose Moran in memory of her mother Bridget Moran who departed this life 15th January 1876 aged 60 years.
(852)

MORAN
Sacred to the memory of Mr. Thomas Moran of Drogheda who died 21st August 1854 in the 36th year of his age. This tribute of respect to his memory was placed here by his afflicted widow Margaret and three of her children who died young and her son John Moran who died 25th June 1842 aged 21 years.

(938)

MORGAN
In memory of Captain Laurence Morgan who died at Liverpool 3rd August 1899 and his son James Bernard died 23rd August 1917. His wife Catherine died 5th September 1930 and their daughter Jane died in 1934.

(359)

MORGAN
Erected by Margaret Morgan of Listoke in memory of her husband Christopher Morgan who died 19th June 1869 also his son Edward died 4th December 1867. Margaret Morgan died 4th February 1889. Catherine Morgan died 9th July 1926 and their daughter Margaret died 19th September 1956.

(407)

MORGAN
Erected by Julia Morgan Steamboat Quay in memory of her mother Margaret Morgan who died 22nd February 1871. May her soul rest in peace. Also the above named Julia who died 1st May 1886 aged 67 years.

(597)

MORGAN
This Stone and Burial Place belongeth to Patt Morgan of Drogheda. Here lieth the bodys of his Father and Mother William and Ann. Also five of his children 1758.

(820)

MORGAN
In memory of Mary the beloved wife of James Morgan who died 5th December 1885 aged 46 years. Also the above named James Morgan who died 20th August 1891 aged 60 years and their son Peter who died 4th May 1897 aged 32 years.

(859)

MORRIS
Erected by Thomas Morris, Mell, in memory of his wife Margaret who died 2nd March 1861 aged 48 years. Also three of their sons who died young.

(895)

MORRIS
See Coffey.

(167)

MOSS
See Whyte.

(454)

MULHOLLAND
Erected by John Mulholland of Drogheda in memory of his father Hugh who died 24th October 1854 aged 67 years. Also Alice wife of the above Hugh died 2nd April 1862 aged 74 years. The above John Mulholland died 23rd February 1869 aged 48 years. Also Charles, son of Hugh who died 29th April 1875 aged 40 years and Nicholas son of Charles who died 23rd April 1880 aged 24 years.
(148)

MULHOLLAND
Erected by Thomas Mulholland, Hardmans Garden in memory of his mother and father.
(289)

MULLAN
Erected by Elizabeth Mullan of Laurence St., Drogheda, in memory of her father Edward Mullan who died 14th June 1850 and her mother Esther Mullan who died 9th February 1872.
(173)

MULLIN
This stone was erected by Mrs. Marcella Mullin of Dublin Gate, Drogheda, in memory of her husband John Mullin who died 11th May 1848 aged 38 years. Also two of their children who died young and their son Daniel O.C. Mullin who died at Texas, America 19th August 1885.
(321)

MULLEN
James Mullen, Greenbatter (This is a piece of broken slate).
(510)

MULLEN
Erected by Mary Mullen, Laurence Gate in memory of her parents and relatives.
(849)

MULQUEEN
See Reynolds.
(441)

MULROY
James Mulroy in memory of his son who died young.
(555)

MULROY
Erected by Edward Mulroy, Laurence Gate in memory of his father Edward who died 5th March 1841 aged 72 years. Also his mother Anne Mulroy died 29th July 1839 aged 51 years. His brother Patrick 11th December 1837 aged 22 years. Also four of his children who died young.
(742)

MULVANY
To the memory of Bernard Mulvany late of North Road who died 3rd October 1872. Also his sister Honora Murphy who died 2nd February 1858 and his sister Bridget Sheridan who died 2nd April 1853 and his niece Catherine Sheridan who died 15th January 1850.
(662)

MURPHY

Erected by Mrs. Mary Murphy of Laurence Gate in memory of her son Michael who departed this life 18th December 1855 aged 25 years and the above Mrs. Mary Murphy who died 1st June 1858 aged 45 years and her daughter Mrs. Mary Kelly who died 8th February 1863 aged 28 years. And her son-in-law Nicholas Anthony Kelly who died 29th October 1867 aged 41 years. Also Peter Joseph Kelly son of the above Nicholas Kelly who died 16th September 1875 aged 17 years and his only daughter Mary Anne Kelly who died September 30th 1875 aged 18 years.

(334)

MURPHY

Of your charity pray for the soul of Mary Anne Murphy, West Street who died 5th March 1879. Her husband James died 6th May 1888 - Augustine Murphy died 14th April 1929. Their daughter Mary Stokes died 9th July 1944 aged 93 years and Anne Murphy who died 28th May 1946.

(208A)

MURPHY

Erected by William Murphy, Mall Mill, Drogheda in memory of his wife Catherine who died 8th October 1861 aged 40 years. Also three of their children Richard, Mary and Francis who died young.

(249)

MURPHY

Pray for the soul of Charles Murphy, Georges Street who died 14th June 1924 and his wife Mary who died 10th January 1955.

(412)

MURPHY

Erected by Thomas Murphy, West Street in memory of his father-in-law George Foskey who died 8th April 1869 aged 56 years and William Thomas son of the above George Foskey who died young. And Deborah wife of Thomas Murphy who died 6th February 1903 aged 58 years and their infant son William H. Murphy who died 25th February 1905. His mother-in law, Maria Foskey, who died 10th February 1910, the above Thomas Murphy died 17th May 1910 and his brother Augustine Murphy who died 14th April 1929.

(415)

MURPHY

This stone is erected by John and Bridget Murphy of William Street, Drogheda, in memory of their dear and beloved daughter Mary who died 21st June 1832 aged 9 years and 6 months. Here also lie the remains of William Garvey grandfather by her mother of the above Mary who died 12th March 1830.

(491)

MURPHY

Erected by Patrick Murphy of Magdalene Street in memory of his father Anthony Murphy who died 1st August 1854 aged 64 years. His mother Jane 10th July 1849 aged 36 years. And his children Anne Jane 18th April 1865 aged 1 year, Anna Maria 1st November 1870 aged 5 years, Anthony Philip 6th November 1870 aged 3 years, Thomas Aloysius 25th October 1880 aged 10 years and Clement ñ infant 23rd November 1882.

(580)

MURPHY
Erected to the memory of Margaret Murphy who died in April 1825 aged 70 years and her daughter Bridget who died 9th October 1842 aged 45 years.

(602)

MURPHY
John Murphy, Hardmans Garden in memory of his son Patrick who died 12th April 1869. His grandfather Patrick Hoey who died in February 1833 and his grandmother Catherine Hoey who died in February 1838 and the above John Murphy died 17th January 1888 aged 68 years. His wife Margaret Murphy died 28th January 1892.

(72)

MURPHY
Erected to the memory of Margaret Murphy who died in April 1825 aged 70 years. Also her daughter Bridget Murphy who died 9th October 1842 aged 70 years.

(862)

MURPHY
Pray for the soul of Hugh Murphy who died 30th January 1881.

MURPHY
See Mulvany.

(662)

MURRAY
Erected to the memory of John Murray of West Gate who departed this life 7th August 1846 aged 64 years. Also three of his children who died young. And his wife Elizabeth who died 6th August 1849 aged 70 years.

(26)

MURRAY
Erected by Mary Murray of Laurence Gate for her husband Michael Murray who died 11th March 1847 aged 57 years.

(27)

MURRAY
Erected by Maryann Murray of Francis Street, Drogheda in memory of her mother Catherine Murray who died 22nd December 1870 aged 70 years and the above Maryann Murray who died 6th March 1884 aged 50 years.

(206)

MURRAY
Owen Murray, Duleek Street, Drogheda.

(467)

MURRAY
Erected by James Murray in memory of his father John who died at his residence Patrick Street, 25th December 1892 aged 78. Also three of his children who died young.

(559)

MURRAY
Sacred to the memory of Patrick Murray who died 16th February 1891 and his father Thomas died 4th March 1893.

(913)

MURRAY
See Kerley.

(573)

MURTAGH
Of your charity pray for the soul of Patrick Murtagh, Governor of the Drogheda Prison who died 27th February 1871 aged 69 years and his wife Margaret died on Ascension Thursday 1872. Here too sleep the remains of John Murtagh who died 19 March 1892 and James W. Murtagh died 11th November 1874, Bernard Murtagh died 11th June 1886 aged 46 years. Margaret died 22nd February 1884 aged 70 years. Doctor Edward Murtagh died 1st March 1887 aged 37 years. Margaret Forstall who died 2nd December 1887 aged 79 years. Margaret Forstall Murtagh died Christmas Day 1895 aged 44 years.

(187)

MURTAGH
This stone was erected by Catherine Murtagh. Here lieth the body of her husband Patrick who died 4th March 1788 aged 52 years. Also seven of his children.

(655)

NEARY
Erected by Michael Neary in memory of his wife Mary who died 27th July 1890 aged 53 years. Also her mother Mary Roe who died 30th March 1890 aged 84 years.

(130)

NEGROSE
See Kelly.

(417)

NEILL
Erected by John Neill to his father Michael who died February 1853.

(276)

NEWGENT
Here lieth the body of Luke Newgent died the 7th February 1784 aged 47 years. This stone was erected by his wife Mary Newgent.

(821)

NOLAN
See Mohan.

(832)

NORRIS
Erected by Bridget Norris in memory of her husband John Norris and his two sons Patrick and Joseph.
(179)

NOTT
Erected to the memory of Mary Nott who died 24th December 1890.
(710)

NUGENT
Erected by Ellen Nugent in memory of her son James who died 5th July 1877 aged 36 years and her son Thomas who died 19th December 1895 aged 48 years.
(154)

NUGENT
Erected by Edward Nugent in memory of his father Owen who died 10th February 1875 aged 82 years and of his brother Bernard who died 10th April 1875 aged 24 years. Also his mother Mary Nugent died 18th July 1882 and Bernard McKenna who died 18th June 1891.
(355)

NUGENT
Erected by Catherine Nugent of West Street, Drogheda in memory of her husband James Nugent who died 29th December 1882 the above Catherine died 9th March 1888.
(549)

NULTY
Erected by Thomas Nulty of Greenhills in memory of his son Patrick Nulty who died 6th August 1846 aged 24 years and the above named Thomas Nulty who died 24th August 1855 and his daughter Mary who died 1st September 1862.
(32)

ODAIR
Erected by Anne Odair in memory of her parents Michael and Mary Loughran and her sister Mary Doyle.
(140)

OGLE
See Kelsh.
(195)

OLWILL
Here lieth the body of Terence Olwill who departed this life 8th of October 1774 aged 39 years. Also three of his children.
(807)

OWENS
Erected by J. Owens, Stockwell Lane in memory of his parents.
(232)

OWENS
Erected by Mr. John Owens of Fair Street, Linen Manufacturer, in memory of his daughter Catherine Owens alias Dullahan who died 10th June 1834 aged 30 years. His son James 18th January 1838 aged 18 years. Thomas Owens 30th April 1842 aged 31 years. The above John Owens 4th December 1854 aged 79 years. His wife Mrs. Mary Owens 24th April 1858 aged 81 years.
(275)

O'BRIEN
Edward O'Brien died 18th February 1881 and his daughter Elisha died 1881.
(115)

O'BRIEN
Erected by Anne O'Brien in memory of her husband John O'Brien who died 3rd February 1885. Also her son James who died 28th February 1892.
(413)

O'BRIEN
Erected by Catherine O'Brien of the Old Abbey in memory of her mother who died 23rd April 1860.
(856)

O'BRINE
Gloria in Excelsis Deo. Erected by Owen O'Brine of Marsh Street, Drogheda to the memory of his wife Catherine who died 26th February 1860 aged 46 years. Also his son James who died in 1845 aged 23 months. And the above Owen died 22nd July 1890 aged 74 years.
(49)

O'CALLAGHAN
Erected by Patrick and Catherine O'Callaghan, 42 Shop Street, Drogheda.
(381)

O'CALLAGHAN
Erected by Patrick O'Callaghan of Shop Street in memory of Barthlemew and Anne Halpin. Also his infant daughter Sarah Jane.
(772)

O'DONEGAN
Erected by John O'Donegan, Bookbinder, in memory of his daughter Catherine and infant son Samuel.
(607)

O'FERRALL
The burial place of Francis O'Ferrall, merchant of Drogheda. Here lies his wife Mary and seven of his children who died young. And the above Francis died 31st December 1893 in the 51st year of his age.

On the reverse side of the stone: "Pray for the soul of Rev–Jn O'Ferrall brother of Francis."
(518)

O'FLAHERTY
Erected by Mary Anne O'Flaherty in memory of her husband Michael who died 19th March 1892 and their son Francis died 11th October 1884. Their daughter Mary Anne died 27th November 1895. The above Mary Anne O'Flaherty who died 6th October 1905.

(426)

O'HALLORAN
Erected by Edward O'Halloran of Trinity Street in memory of his wife Elizabeth who died 11th January 1882 aged 68 years and the above Edward died 29th January 1888 aged 82 years.

(119A)

O'HARE
In memory of Jane, wife of Andrew O'Hare, Scarlet Street who died October 23rd 1874 and their daughter Elisha Savage who died March 17th 1876. Also their children John and Mary Ann who died young.

(74)

O'MALLEY
Mary O'Malley erected this stone in memory of her father and mother Laurence and Mary Traynor.

(234)

O'NEIL
Erected by Paul O'Neil of Drogheda to the memory of his brother Bernard an honest good tobacco spinner who died 15th February 1812 aged 74 years. Also for him and his posterity.

(745)

O'NEILL
Erected by Anne O'Neill of Marsh Road in memory of her husband Francis who died 4th May 1877 and their daughter Anne who died young.

(201A)

O'NEILL
Erected by Henry O'Neill in memory of his wife Mary who died 10th August 1878 aged 70 years and his son Patrick who died 4th December 1877 aged 43 years.

(514)

O'NEILL
Erected to the memory of Elizabeth O'Neill of the Old Hill who died July 1890 aged 75 years. Her husband John O'Neill died 17th September 1869 aged 67 years.

(748)

O'NEILL
Erected by James O'Neill in memory of his mother Catherine O'Neill who died 19th February 1876 aged 74 years.

(942)

O'REILLY
Here lie the mortal remains of John O'Reilly and of Marcella Ternan otherwise O'Reilly, his sister. This stone was erected to the memory of both by their only surviving brother in the year of our Lord 1800.

(756)

O'REILLY
See Grady.
(516)

O'REILLY
See Carney.
(160)

O'ROURKE
Richard O'Rourke of Blackbutt Lane, Drogheda in memory of his son Nicholas died March 2nd 1857 aged 20 years.
(878)

O'SHEA
See Sisters of Charity.
(1)

O'TOOLE
See Anderson.
(197)

PALMER
Erected in memory of John Thomas Palmer, Cord Road who died 12th June 1883 aged 65 years. Also eight of his children who died young and his wife Mary who died 11th November 1907.
(83)

PATTERSON
Here lieth the body of Mrs. Mary Patterson, wife of Mr. James Patterson, who died 12th day of September 1788 in the 41st year of her age.
(517)

PENTLAND
Erected by Surgeon and Mrs. Pentland to the memory of Mrs. Carty a faithful servant and valued friend. She died in her 80th year at their residence on the 10th of March 1853.
(29)

PENTONY
See Magrane.
(101)

PICKETT
Erected by Anne Picket, North Road in memory of her sister Mary Cusack who died 1st January 1883.
(72)

PLUNKET
Erected by Thomas Plunket of Green Hills in memory of his son Joseph who died 11th October 1885 aged 24 years and eight other of his children who died young. Also his father and mother-in-law James and Honor McEvoy of James's Street.

(557)

PLUNKETT
This stone and burial place belongeth to Patt Plunkett of Drogheda 1770.

(713)

PLUNKETT
See McDonnell.
This is a rough cut stone with the two letters, P.L. cut near the top.

(864)

PORTER
See Gorman

(614)

POUGE
Erected by James Pouge of Trinity Street, Drogheda in memory of his parents Thomas & Rose Pouge, his brother Andrew, his sisters Mary & Anne, his brother Thomas who died 7th June 1891 aged (blank) years.

(490)

POWDERLY
Erected by Mathew Powderly of Sundays Gate, Drogheda in memory of his father Edward who died 10th January 1840 aged 42 years. His mother Mary died 12th March 1866 aged 72 years. His brother and sister who died young.

(703)

PRIESTLY
Sacred to the memory of Bridget the dearly beloved wife of George Priestly who died 10th September 1878 and their infant children Mary Jane and George Francis.

(3)

PURCEL
Erected by John Prucel of Drogheda in memory of his wife Mary who died 11th August 1828 aged 60 years. Also his brother James Purcel who died in May 1789 aged 30 years. Also his daughter Catherine who died young. The above John Purcel died 16th July 1842 aged 75 years. Also his brother Richard.

(575)

QUAIL
In memory of Elizabeth Quail who died 9th April 1861 aged 72 years. Her son Peter died 28th April 1871 aged 50 years and Peter infant son of Mathew Walsh and nephew of the above who died 10th July 1871 aged 14 days.

(77)

QUIGLEY
Erected by Anne Quigley in memory of her husband Thomas Quigley and family.

(949)

QUINN
Erected by John Quinn, New Dublin Road, Drogheda, in memory of his father Patrick Quinn who died 1st December 1826 aged 59 years. Also two of his children who died young. His mother Anne Quinn died 21st January 1856. John Quinn 9th March 1877. Catherine Quinn 9th October 1881.

(802)

QUINN
See Dowdall.

(518)

QUINN
See Moran.

(629)

RAFFERTY
Erected by John Rafferty in memory of his mother Anne died 1851, his father Bernard died 1852, his wife Anne died 30th August 1889, his daughter Alice died 29th December 1888. The above John Rafferty died 20th August 1891 aged 57 years.

(519)

RAFFERTY
See Falconer.

(860)

READ
Also James Read, Sunday Gate grandson by marriage of the Ajoint Sarah Brown who died 6th September 1829 aged 42 years. Also Sarah Read wife of the above James Read 12th May 1858 aged 46 years. Her grandchildren Sarah, James and Lizzy McKenna who died young.

(633)

REARDON
This monument was raised by Mrs. Sarah Reardon of Windmill Cottage, Drogheda in memory of her husband Michael who departed this life on the 26th day of June 1852 aged 51 years. He was the late Sub Inspector of Constabulary in Drogheda.

(188)

REDDY
Erected by Ellen Reddy, Laurence Street in memory of her parents Andrew and Mary Reddy. Also the above Ellen who died 4th May 1888 aged 60 years.

(220)

REID
Erected by Catherine Reid in memory of her mother Dora Egan who died 12th September 1877.
(172)

REID
Erected by Mr. John Reid of the town of Sligo in memory of his mother Margaret Reid who departed this life 12th June 1861 aged 56 years.
(562)

REID
Erected by Nicholas Reid, Carntown, in memory of his children Mary Anne who died 3rd January 1872 aged 17 years. John died 3rd August 1875 aged 16 years. The above Nicholas Reid died 13th January 1886 aged 68 years.
(658)

REILLY
Erected by Peter Reilly, West Street, Drogheda in memory of his beloved wife Annie Bridget who died 21st September 1880.
(21)

REILLY
Sacred to the memory of Charles Reilly, Black Bull who died 5th June 1894. His wife Rose who died 10th June 1894 and their daughter Margaret who died 2nd August 1881.
(37)

REILLY
Erected by Patrick Reilly of King Street in memory of his father and mother.
(144)

REILLY
Judith and James Reilly, Johns Gate, Drogheda.
(216)

REILLY
Your prayers are requested for the happy repose of the soul of Catherine, the beloved wife of Thomas Reilly of Mell, who died 28th December 1881 aged 34 years and their nine children who all died young.
(225)

REILLY
Erected 1853 by Patrick Reilly of West Gate, Drogheda in memory of his wife Dorothy who died 13th June 1853 aged 27 years. Also her daughters Anne who died 8th May 1854 aged two years and Bridget who died 23rd November 1861 aged 12 years. Also to the memory of his mother-in-law Mary McCullough who died 17th December 1868 aged 70 years. Of your Charity pray for the happy repose of the soul of the above Patrick Reilly who died 4th September 1879 aged 67 years.
(301)

REILLY
Erected by James Reilly of Trinity Street in memory of his brother Richard Reilly who died 1st November 1888.
(387)

REILLY
Sacred to the memory of John and Mary Reilly, Ship Street.
(435)

REILLY
To the memory of Miss Jane Reilly who departed this life 5th of March 1837 in the 18th year of her age. This stone was placed here to her memory by her brother-in-law Mr. John Savage of Drogheda.
(542)

REILLY
Erected AD.1863 by Philip Reilly, Duke Street, Drogheda, in memory of his father Edward Reilly who died 12th June 1856 aged 53 years and his mother Margaret Reilly who died 10th November 1859 aged 50 years. Also his sister Alice Reilly who died 10th November 1860 aged 15 years. And also his brother Patrick Reilly who died 6th October 1861 aged 17 years. Also his brother Edward 17th January 1865 aged 24 years and the above Philip died 1st January 1870 and his nephew John Culloden who died young.
(779)

REILLY
Erected by John Reilly of Drogheda for him and his posterity. Also two of his children who died young.
(951)

REILLY
See Carolan.
(547)

REILLY
See McDonnell.
(770)

REILLY
See Fitzsimons.
(775)

REILY
See McClain.
(720)

REYNOLDS
Erected by Frank Reynolds M.E., Bredin Street in memory of his father Captain William Reynolds of the Barque *Salus* who was drowned at Buenos Ayres 10th June 1882 aged 41 years. His mother Annie died 13th March 1905 aged 64 years and their three children, also two grandchildren and his sisters Anastasia Mulqueen died 22nd June 1933 aged 63 years and Mary Jane died 1st May 1946 and the above Frank died 6th November 1960.
(441)

REYNOLDS
Erected by Catherine Reynolds, Bull Ring, in memory of her husband Peter Reynolds who died 8th April 1891 aged 66 years. Also Joseph who died young.

(442)

REYNOLDS
Erected by John Reynolds, John Street, Drogheda in memory of his dear parents his wife and children and other relatives whose remains are interred here. The above John Reynolds died 17th July 1886 aged 76 years.

(700)

RICE
Patrick Rice late of Magdalene Street who died 29th October 1884.

(36)

RICE
Erected by Michael Rice, Castledermot, County Kildare in memory of his wife Mary Elizabeth who died 3rd October 1860 in the 23rd year of her age.

(41)

RICE
Erected by Ellen Rice of Drogheda in memory of her beloved husband Patrick Rice who departed this life 3rd March 1850 aged 38 years. Also her daughter Bridget who died young. Also her son Michael Rice died 5th May 1863 aged 19 years. Judith Rice died June 6th 1863. Also the above named Ellen Rice died May 4th 1879.

(121)

RICE
Erected by John Rice of Patrick Street, Drogheda in memory of his son William Rice who died 27th of August 1843 aged 28 years.

(132)

RICE
Erected by Sarah Rice, Marsh, in memory of her father John Rice who died November 1855 aged 62 years. Also her mother Margaret Rice who died December 1856 aged 60 years.

(957)

RICHARDS
See Byrne.

(869)

RIELY
Erected by Bernard Riely of Magdalene Street in memory of his father Hugh Riely who died 26th March 1835 aged 66 years. And his mother Mary Riely who died 31st March 1836 aged 56 years. Also his sister Mary Riely who died December 29th 1850 aged 57 years.

(847)

RIELLY
Erected by Richard Rielly of Drogheda in memory of his wife Christina who died 15th July 1849 aged 36 years.

> Mourn not for me I am dead and gone
> My loving husband Gods will be done
> And on my children pity take
> And care them for their Mother's sake.

Also his brother Charles who died 5th September 1841 aged 34 years.

(560)

RIELLY
Erected by Mary Anne Rielly of Peter Street, Drogheda, to the memory of her beloved husband Michael Rielly who departed this life 11th of June 1850 aged 48 years.

(935)

ROBINSON
Erected by Thomas Robinson of Thomas Street in memory of his mother Anne Robinson died 1st November 1842 aged 70 years. Also his brother John died June 1830 aged 37 years.

(533)

RODGERS
Erected by James Rodgers in memory of his father Patrick Rodgers who died in November 1825.

(839)

RODGERS
Erected by Peter Rodgers, Ship Street, Drogheda in memory of his father John Rodgers who died 14th June 1866 also his mother Bridget Rodgers who died 2nd February 1873, also his son who died young.

(923)

RODGERS
See Duffy.

(837)

ROE
Here lieth the body of Peter Roe who departed this life the 9th of May 1739 aged 49 years. Also ten of his children.

(717)

ROE
See Neary.

(130)

ROIGE
See Sisters of Charity.

(1)

ROONEY
Erected by Richard Rooney of Rathmullen in memory of his wife Roas Rooney.
(666)

ROURKE
Erected by John Rourke, Duleek Street in memory of his brother-in-law Darby Keogh who died 31st August 1884 aged 40 years and his son John died 15th June 1883 aged 22 years.
(446)

RUSSELL
Erected by Michael Russell AD 1874 in memory of his father and mother Thomas and Anne Russell, Newfoundwell.
(525)

RYAN
P. Ryan.
(823)

RYELY
This stone and burial place belongs to Thomas Ryely of Drogheda. Underneath lieth the body of Meable Ryely the above Thomas his daughter who departed this life the 17th of April in the year 1760 aged 13 years.
(492)

SAMPSON
Erected by James Sampson, Duleek Street in memory of his father James Sampson who died 8th June 1864 aged 86 years and his sister Margaret who died young. Also his wife Mary Anne died 13th January 1895 aged 50 years.
(622)

SAVAGE
See O'Hare.
(74)

SAVAGE
See Reilly.
(542)

SEGRAVE
Erected by Mary Segrave, Scarlet Street, in memory of her husband Michael who died 6th November 1903 aged 43 and their daughter Nannie who died 2nd August 1902.
(458)

(Death Insertion, *'Drogheda Independent'* 20th October 1981.)
SEGRAVE: (Drogheda) 15th October 1981 at Our Lady of Lourdes Hospital, Drogheda, Mary Segrave, 9 St. Finian's Park; deeply regretted by her loving daughters, brother, sister, sons-in-law, grandchildren, relatives and friends. R.I.P. Mass in Holy Family Church, Ballsgrove on Saturday 17th October at 11 o'clock. Funeral took place immediately afterwards to Cord Cemetery.

SCOTT
See Clifford.

(348)

SHAW
Mary Shaw of Green Lanes in memory of her husband John Shaw who died 30th September 1885 and four children who died young.

(107)

SHEKLETON
Erected by Rose Shekleton of Drogheda in memory of her husband Nicholas who died 22nd December 1861 aged 60 years.

(58)

SHERIDAN
Erected by Patrick Sheridan, West Gate in memory of his wife Margaret who died 27th February 1861 aged 67 years. Also their son Hugh who died 14th June 1864 aged 35 years the above Patrick Sheridan died 9th February 1865 aged 68 years.

(129)

SHERIDAN
Erected by Anne Sheridan in memory of her daughter Catherine who died 14th March 1892 and Bridget who died young.

(485)

SHERIDAN
See Mulvany.

(662)

SHERLOCK
Erected by John Sherlock of Duleek Street in memory of his brother Patrick who died 17th December 1883 aged 72 years.

(312)

SHERRY
Erected AD 1814 by Dorothy Sherry in memory of her father and mother Thomas and May Byrne and six of their children. Here also lieth the body of her daughter Elizabeth McCuillin who died 13th October 1813 aged 24 years and one infant and also four children of the above.

(774)

SHERRY
Sacred to the memory of Hugh Sherry who died 18th December 1880 aged 82 years and his wife Judith who died 18th June 1858 aged 48 years.

(168)

SHERRY
Erected by Owen Sherry of Green Hills in memory of his wife Mary Sherry who departed this life 1st November 1846 aged 61 years.
(219)

SHEIL
Erected to the memory of Hugh Sheil who died 26th March 1860 aged 46 years. And his mother Judith Sheil who died 18th July 1864 aged 72 years.
(521)

SHIELS
Erected by William Shiels, mason, in memory of his son James who died 22nd June 1847 aged 19 years. Also his daughter Catherine who died young. Also his daughter Eliza who died 5th October 1851 aged 16 years. Also his wife Catherine Shiels who died 4th November 1861 aged 60 years and the above William Shiels who died the 8th of February 1864 aged 66 years and Mrs. Jane Conn daughter of the above William and Catherine Shiels died 24th January 1891 aged 56 years.
(100)

SHIELS
Erected by Mary Shiels in loving memory of her husband Capt. Thomas Shiels, Greenhills who died 31st March 1918 and of their sons William died 26th March 1885. John died 14th may 1898. Thomas died 18th April 1906. Also the above Mary Shiels who died 30th July 1921 and of their daughter Kate Martin died 17th September 1922 and Annie Shiels died 3rd October 1949.
(347)

SHIELS
See Levins.
(401)

SHORT
Erected by Michael Short of Wicklow in memory of his beloved children Bridget and John aged respectively 10 and 3 years and his sister Mary.
(596)

SHORT
Erected by Patrick Short of Drogheda in memory of his wife Mary who died in 1825 aged 26 years. Also three of his children who died young.
(879)

SHORT
See Kennedy.
(536)

SHUEMAN
'Erected by Mrs. Kate Shueman in memory of her dearly beloved husband Thomas Shueman who departed this life 1st February 1875'.
(In September 1973 the above inscription was taken from a marble plaque which was moved down to the church vaults – for safe keeping).

SIMCOCKS
Erected by Thomas Simcocks of West Street, Drogheda in memory of his father Thomas who died 5th March 1857 aged 72 years. Also his brother Gerald Simcocks who died 1st May 1857 aged 32 years and his wife Mary Simcocks who died 18th December 1875 in the 56th year of her age.

(307)

SIMCOCKS
See Healy.

(22)

SIMINGTON
In loving memory of Sarah died 3rd July 1888, Joseph – 4th November '89, Ida – 30th April '98 and their father P.J. Simington died 16th December 1902. Also their mother Johanna Mary died 31st August 1912.

(424)

SIMINGTON
See Kelly.

(452)

SISTERS OF CHARITY

Spes Unica..

Sister Mary O'Shea	died 7th November 1863 aged 35.
Sister T. Lucy Roice	died 8th August 1873 aged 39.
Sister C. Anne Boylan	died 9th July 1876 aged 44.
Sister F. Carroll	died 14th August 1879 aged 25.
Sister C. Golden	died 12th September 1879 aged 30.
Sister J. Ginnety	died 12th October 1880 aged 39.
Sister A. O'Shea	died 20th March 1886 aged 34.
Sister T. Duffy	died 21st August 1888 aged 40.

(The above were translated to St. Peter's Cemetery, Drogheda on 8th August 1980. See St. Peter's Cemetery, 1993 by James Garry p83 which shows the full Christian names of these nuns).

(1)

SISTERS OF CHARITY
Erected by the Sisters of Charity to the memory of Mary King who died 16th November 1872.

(841)

SKELLY
Erected by Thomas Skelly in memory of his son Patrick who died 2nd April 1851 aged 8 years.

(255)

The Grave in St. Peter's Cemetery to which the remains of eight nuns were translated in 1980

SKELLY
See Boylan.
(479)

SLATOR
This stone and burial place belongeth to John Slator, merchant in Drogheda. Here lyeth two of his children 1776.
(592)

SLEVIN
Erected by James Slevin, Fair Street, in memory of his family. Here lieth the remains of three of his children. Anne, Peter and Mary who died young. Also his daughter Ellen who departed this life 5th August 1852 in the 12th year of her age. His wife Anne Slevin died 7th July 1865 age 46 years. The above James Slevin died 2nd August 1873 aged 60 years.
(725)

SMITH
Erected by Mary Smith in memory of her parents John and Bessie Smith.
(122)

SMITH
Erected by Patrick Smith, Railway Terrace in memory of his children Thomas Francis who died 19th December 1870 aged 21 years and Henry who died 29th January 1880 aged 4 years.
(127)

SMITH
Erected by James Smith in memory of his wife Anne who died 30th October 1885 aged 50 years. Also his daughter Mary who died 28th April 1887 aged 22 years.
(134)

SMITH
Erected by Patrick Smith of Bolton Street in memory of his sons Patrick who died 12th October 1869 aged 20 years and James who died 12th March 1875 aged 18 years.
(162)

SMITH
Erected by Mary Anne Smith, Mary Street in memory of her husband Frederick Smith who died 24th December 1867.
(177)

SMITH
Erected by Patrick Smith, Livens Bridge, Drogheda, in memory of his father and mother and his brother David Smith AD 1870. The above Patrick Smith died 1880 and his son Andrew 19th February 1884.
(204A)

SMITH
Daughter of Patrick Smith, West Street died 14th February '92 aged 19 years. His parents three brothers and two sisters are also interred here. R.I.P.
(Top of this stone is broken).
(288)

SMITH
Sacred to the memory of John Smith, Hardmans Garden, who died 31st January 1855 aged 45 years. His wife Anne 8th October 1882 aged 84 years.

(292)

SMITH
In memory of Mary Anne Smith, Dale died 11th January 1900 her father Michael died 23rd November 1907.

(463)

SMITH
Erected by James Smith in memory of his mother Elizabeth Smith who died at Duleek Street, Drogheda 14th October 1867 aged 30 years. His brothers John 4th September 1865 aged 15 years and Michael who died young.

(556)

SMITH
In memory of Bridget Smith of Duleek Street who died 1st September 1878 aged 21 years. On whose soul sweet Jesus have mercy.

(794)

SMITH
To the memory of Mary Smith who died 19th December 1869 aged 70 years. Also Sarah Dunne age two years and John Laurence Dunne aged 16 years grandchildren of the above.

(846)

SMITH
Erected by Owen Smith of Drogheda.

Low here dose lie relas,d from worly care
The dear remains of a sweet lovly fair
Whose sole desire was plas,d in heaven above
Her God alone was all her Joy and Love.
Her happy life was one continued scene
of Prayer devotion vertue and esteem.
of her sweet lord and heavens bright
                queenlike wife.
Till her dear soul did soar above the skeys
There evermore to sing eternal praise
To her good God and bless his glororious way.
As she has done when in this life confind
But now her voice is treble more refind
Just in the eleventh year of her age
This child of God dropt off this mortal stage
And bid adue to this frail world of sin
Where no real joy is to be had within.

So much to the memory of Ann Smith
daughter of the above Owen Smith
She died June the 21st 1818
Also his son Peter he died in the 5th
year of his age.

(890)

SMITH
Erected by Mrs. Lizzie Smith of the Marsh in memory of her son Patrick J. Smith who died 14th November 1886 aged 27 years.

(894)

SMITH
See Martin.

(509)

SMITH
See Farrell.

(915)

SMYTH
Erected by Thomas Smyth in memory of his mother Catherine who died 4th September 1881 and his father Charles who died 1st January 1889.

(120)

SMYTH
Pray for the soul of Patrick Smyth who died 16th January 1896 his wife Bridget died 24th February 1918.

(483)

SMYTH
See McKenna.

(792)

SNOW
Erected A.D.1850 by John Snow of North Strand, Drogheda to mark the spot where rest the mortal remains of his beloved wife Mary in whom was combined every Virtue calculated to make her beloved and respected. She died 22nd September 1842 in the 35th year of her age. Here also lieth her daughter Catherine Snow who died 22nd December 1824 aged 14 years.

(799)

STANLEY
Erected by Thomas Stanley, Cord Road, Drogheda in memory of his two sons Patrick died 29th March 1877 and Thomas died 22nd August 1879.

(368)

STEPHENS
Erected by William Stephens, Blackbull, in memory of his wife Rose who died 6th June 1881 aged 54 years.

(531)

STEWARD
Erected by Eliza Steward of West Street, Drogheda in memory of her husband Matthew Steward who died 25th December 1838 aged 29 years.

(941)

STEWARD
See McCormack.

(105)

STOKES
See Murphy.

(208A)

SULLIVAN
Erected by Patrick Sullivan in memory of his beloved children, Ellen & Eugene who died 21st November 1875 aged 3 years and 2 months and Martin William died 27th November 1875 aged 1 year and 10 months.

(881)

SULLIVAN
See Markey.

(445)

-------------------------------- SURNAME MISSING
Also his beloved daughter Margaret who died March 1864 aged 22 years and his wife Anne who died 2nd February 1873 aged 60 years.

(777)

SWEENEY
Erected by Bernard Sweeney in memory of his children who died young.

(486)

SWEENEY
Lord have mercy on the soul of Myles Sweeney 1852.

(769)

SWEENEY
Erected to the memory of Mr. James Sweeney of Drogheda who died 19th February 1851 in the 68th year of his age.

(870)

SWIFT
In memory of James J. Swift died 12th February 1901 also his wife Jane Francis died 16th July 1921.

(362)

TAAFFEE
Erected by Nicholas Taaffe of Prospect Avenue, in memory of his wife Jane Taaffe who died 26th April 1871 aged 44 years, also two of their children who died young.
(827)

TALLEN
Sacred to the memory of Michael Tallen of the Potatoe Market, who died 29th June 1873 aged 40 year.
(786)

TALLON
Erected by Thomas Tallon, Laurence Street, in memory of his father Patrick Tallon who died 7th March 1879 aged 70 years and his sister Mary Horne who died 6th November 1899 and the said Thomas Talon who died 4th January 1907. Finian Henry Tallon M.R.I.A.I.G.E. 3rd son of the above Thomas who died 19th June 1908 aged 27 years. Mary Ann widow of the above died 12th November 1912.
(369)

TANDY
See Callaghan.
(14)

TEELING
September 1805. Here lieth the body of Patrick Teeling, also his wife and five of his children.
(530)

TEELING
Erected by Thomas Teeling of Drogheda in memory of his mother Anne Teeling who died 8th April 1821 aged 62 years. His father Patrick Teeling died 10th January 1822 aged 61 years and also his sister Catherine.
(955)

TERNAN
See O'Reilly.
(756)

TERNEY
John Terney of Mell erected this in memory of his mother Catherine 29th October 1859 aged 60 years and her step-father Peter Carroll who died 16th June 1856 aged 53 years.
(60)

THIRD ORDER OF ST. FRANCIS
I.H.S. Have the Charity to pray for the souls of the deceased members of the Third Order of St. Francis whose bodies are interred here. It is a holy and a wholesome thought to pray for the dead that they may be loosed from sins – 12 MACABEES 46V.
(337)

THIRD ORDER OF ST. DOMINICK
This monument has been erected by the members of the Chapter of the Third Order of Saint Dominick of Linen Hall Street Chapel in the memory of their deceased brothers and sisters whose remains are deposited within these precincts.
(227)

THOMAS
See Dominican Nuns.

THORNTON
Erected by Patrick Thornton, Duke Street in memory of his wife Jane who died 24th May 1879. Also Maria McEntegart who died 9th April 1881 and his son Joseph who died 12th March 1893.

(648)

THORNTON
Erected by Henry Thornton of Patrick Street, Drogheda in memory of his father Richard who died 2nd December 1840 aged 60 years. Also his son Charles who died 20th March 1867 aged 18 years and the above Henry Thornton died 11th March 1873 aged 52 years.

(948)

TIERNAN
Erected by Anne Tiernan of Bolton Street in memory of her father Owen Brennan who died 6th September 1874 aged 78 years. And the above Anne Tiernan who died 4th August 1881 aged 45 years. Mary Brennan died 22nd November 1882.

(595)

TIERNEY
See Brown.

(634)

TIERNEY
See Courteney.

(627)

TIGHE
Patrick Tighe of North Road in memory of his wife Judith.

(277)

TIMMONS
Erected by Mary Timmons to the memory of her parents Thomas Timmons died 5th December 1871 and Mary Timmons 2nd September 1866. Also her brother Richard Timmons who died 19th June 1891.

(635)

TOKER
Erected by Capt. Edward Toker in memory of his uncle Edward Cahill who died in the year 1834 and his brother James Toker who died in the same year. Also his brother Peter Toker who died 23rd June 1859.

(809)

TOKER
Erected by Capt. Edward Toker in memory of his father James Toker who died in the year 1826. Also his mother Mary died in 1832. His son William Toker who died in Calcutta January 1867 aged 25 years

and five of his children who died young. Also his wife Ellen died 5th June 1883 aged 67 years and the above named Capt. Edward Toker died January 1885 aged 69 years.

(810)

TOKER
Erected by Capt. Edward Toker in memory of his grandfather and grandmother who lie underneath. Also his aunt Mrs. Jane McCoy who died 16th June 1867 aged 87 years.

(811)

TONER
And again, when he bringeth in the 1st begotten into the world, He saith, and let all the angels of God worship Him. Hebrew Chap. 1 Verse 6.

Erected by Michael Toner of Townrath in memory of his father Pat Toner who died March the 2nd 1792 aged 62 years. Also his brother James Toner who died September the 28th 1813 aged 24. And his brother's son Michael Toner who died June the 15th 1811 aged 8 years. Here also lies the remains of his mother Mary Toner otherwise McCann who died 25th of August 1820 aged 72 years. *(This stone depicts The Nativity of Our Lord and is signed by P. Corigan).*

(709)

TONER
Erected by James Toner of Townrath in memory of his wife Judith Toner who died 18th March 1860 aged 55 years. Also his daughter Bridget who died 14 June 1862 aged 13 years.

(851)

TRAYNOR
See O'Malley.

(234)

TRAYNOR
See Treanor.

(760)

TREACY
Erected by Matthew Treacy in memory of his wife Ann Treacy who died 24th February 1870 aged 45 years and the above Matthew Treacy died 20th October 1887 aged 65 years.

(893)

TREANOR
Erected AD.1855 by John Treanor of Laurence Gate in memory of his father Anthony Treanor who died 17th February 1827 aged 45 years. Also his mother Mary who died 16th July 1849 aged 51 years and his sister Bridget who died 24th May 185- age 33 years. The above John Traynor died 4th December 1867 and his daughter Mary 20th January 1871 and his nephew Peter Kain was killed in Dublin 8th November 1880.

(760)

TRINOR
This stone was erected by Patrick Trinor of Drogheda where underneath lyeth —- his children.

(541)

TUITE
This stone was erected AD.1822 by William Tuite of Drogheda for him and his Posterity. Here lieth the body of his mother Bridget Tuite who departed this life 4th of July 1778 aged 56 years. Here also is the body of his father John Tuite who died 24th October 1820 aged 64 years.
(259)

TULLY
Erected 1885 by Margaret Tully in memory of her dear mother and sister Bridget and Mary Tully.
(57)

TULLY
Erected by Peter Tully of West Gate, Drogheda to his wife Bridget who died 5th May 1872 aged 44 years. And their three children who died young. And their son Patrick who died 17th June 1886 aged 24 years.
(323)

TULLY
Erected by Judith Tully of West Gate, Drogheda in memory of her husband John Tully who died 28th April 1846 aged 57 years. Also the above Judith who died 8th December 1853 aged 63 years. Here also is the remains of Thomas Tully son of the above John and Judith who died 18th November 1869 aged 47 years. Also her son Peter who died 6th January 1889 aged 68.
(324)

TUMALTY
Erected by Anne Tumalty of Green Lanes in memory of her husband Richard Tumalty who died 20th March 1873 aged 62 years, their son James who died 25th July 1876 aged 34 years and four of their children who died young.
(145)

TYRRELL
See Daly.
(366)

VERDON
Erected by Catherine Verdon, West Street, in memory of her husband Thomas Verdon who died 15th November 1875 aged 65 years. Also their grand daughter Mary AnneDowdall who died 28th September 1876 aged 18 years. The above named Catherine Verdon died 26th May 1886 aged 73 years.
(503)

WADE
Daniel Wade of Philadelphia erected this in memory of his father John Wade of Green Lanes who died 10th January 1881 and his mother Grace died 6th January 1894. Also his brother Francis died 20th October 1894 aged 38 years.
(922)

WALLACE
Erected AD.1849 by Patrick Wallace of Magdalene Street, Drogheda. Here are interred two of his children who died young. And the above Patrick who died 15th September 1850 aged 12 years.

(206A)

WALLACE
Erected by William Wallace in memory of his brother-in-law ISAAC JOSEPH WEBB who died 17th December 1871 aged 76 years and Thomas son of I.J. WEBB who died 28th November 1876 aged 18 years.

(238)

WALIRON
To the memory of Mr. John Waliron late of Drogheda who died 2nd July 1831 in the 35th year of his age. This tribute of respect to the memory of an affectionate and industrious husband has been placed here by his mourning widow Mary. Also the remains of Mrs. MI. Moore who died 17th May 1832 sister of the above Mr. John Waliron.

(566)

WALIRIN
Sacred to the memory of Mr. Simon Walirin of Stockwell Lane, Tanner, who departed this life 25th June 1860.

(567)

WALSH
Sacred to the memory of Peter Walsh who departed this life 22nd October 1869 aged 64 years and his wife Mary who died 22nd of April 1882 aged 80 years and their daughter Catherine who died 13th October 1859 aged 15 years. Also their son John who died 2nd of November 1886 aged 45 years.

(9)

WALSH
Erected by John Walsh in memory of his infant daughter Mary Anne who died 5th December 1877.

(171)

WALSH
Erected by Patrick Walsh in memory of his son Patts died 1857. Also his daughter Elizabeth died 1871 and Mary died 1876.

(504)

WALSH
Of your charity pray for the soul of Cathering Walsh who died 3rd December 1869 aged 62 years. Also Michael Walsh husband of the above who died 18th December 1869 aged 71 years. Also Patrick Walsh son of the above who died 3rd April 1870 aged 42 years. Also John Walsh brother of Michael died 10th January 1870 aged 70 years.

(587)

WALSH
Erected to the memory of Mr. Thomas Walsh, West Street, Merchant who departed this life March 1826 aged 78 years. Also Bridget his beloved wife who died 17th September 1858. Also Mary Walsh the only child of the above and the dearly beloved wife of Michael Crinnon who died 1st April 1811 aged 41 years.

(706)

WALSH
Here lyeth the body of Mary Walsh wife of Mr. Grahan who deyed December ye 10th 1741 aged 21 years.

(812)

WALSH
Erected by John Walsh of Drogheda, Skinner, in memory of his father Oliver Walsh who died 22nd of March 1787 aged 42 years. Also his mother Anne Walsh who died 3rd July 1800 aged 56 years.

(813)

WALSH
Erected by Elizabeth Walsh of Millmount Terrace, in memory of her father Michael Walsh who died 16th May 1851 aged 68 years. Also her mother Rose Walsh who died 8th January 1866 aged 84 years and her brother Michael Walsh died 16th April 1879 aged 60 years.

(854)

WALSH
See Quail.

(77)

WALSH
See Gaffney.

(231)

WALSH
See Winne.

(550)

WATERS
In memory of Esther Waters who died 7th May 1897.

(432)

WATERS
Erected by Margaret Waters, Levins Bridge, Drogheda in memory of her husband Nicholas Waters who died 14th August 1873. The above Margaret Waters died 11th May 1895.

(534)

WATSON
Erected by Catherine Watson in memory of her husband Bernard Watson who died 13th December 1886, also her mother.
(866)

WARREN
Erected by Michael Warren, North Road, in memory of his wife Bridget died 15th August 1867.
(246)

WEBB
See Wallace.
(238)

WELDON
Erected by Patrick Weldon, Fair Street, Drogheda, in memory of his mother Anne Weldon who died 2nd July 1884. And his son Michael who died young. The above Patrick Weldon died 25th July 1905 and his wife Anne who died 14th October 1924.
(419)

WHELAN
Erected by Michael Whelan of Dyer Street in memory of his wife Susan who died November 1853 aged 56 years and Catherine who died 5th August 1880 aged 72 years.
(67)

WHELAN
In memory of Julia Whelan, Bredin Street who died 19th February 1911, her husband James died 6th October 1917. John Whelan died 20th January 1931 aged 50 years. His brother James died 6th March 1953.
(430)

WHERLY
See McClain.
(720)

WHEARTY
See McCullough.
(114)

WHERTY
Erected by John Wherty of Hand Street in memory of his father James who died 20th June 1875 and his mother Mary died 25th November 1877.
(738)

WHITE
Pray for Alice White 1842.
(310)

WHITE
Erected by Henry White of Drogheda, Linen Manufacturer, in memory of his father Nicholas White

who died 7th November 1768 aged 44 years. Also his mother Margaret White who died March 1785 aged 56 years.

(544)

WHITE
Erected by Mr. Nicholas White of West Street, Drogheda in memory of his wife Barbara who died 6th May 1831 aged 33 years. Also the above Nicholas White died 3rd December 1847 in the 44th year of his age.

(667)

WHITE
Erected by Charles White of Drogheda in memory of his daughter Margaret who departed this life 10th July 1832 aged 33 years.

(927)

WHITE
See McKenna.

(792)

WHITEHEAD
Erected by Patrick Whitehead of Scarlet Street, Drogheda in memory of his daughter Margaret who died 16th December 1860 aged 13 years. His son Owen died at sea 21st August 1870 aged 25 years. His grand-child Mary A. Flanagan died 13th March 1866 aged 2½ years. The above Patrick Whitehead died 15th May 1890 aged 80 years.

(637)

WHITEHEAD
See Flanagan.

(453)

WHYTE
To the memory of Francis Whyte, Thomas Street who died 21st March 1889 aged 62 years and his wife Ellen who died 15th June 1895 aged 68 years. Also their nephew Francis Moss who died 25th January 1896 aged 29 years.

(454)

WINNE
This stone and burial place belongeth to Patrick Winne of Drogheda and his posterity. Here lieth two of his children who died in their infancy Anno Domine 1781. Renewed by Richard Walsh son-in-law of the above Patrick in memory of his sons John and Thomas the former died 20th may 1844 aged 6 years, the latter died 30th June 1862 aged 16 years.

(550)

WISDOM
See McKowne.

(822)

WOODLOCK
This monument was erected by Mrs. Margaret Woodlock of James Street, Drogheda,, in memory of her daughter Mrs. Johanna Butterly who died 26th September 1852 in the 34th year of her age.

(661)

WOODS
Mr. Thomas Woods of Laurence Gate erected this to his wife Bridget Woods who departed this life 4th December 1848 aged 32 years. And the above Thomas Woods died 13th October 1867 aged 60 years.

(221)

WOODS
IN MEMORY OF JAMES WOODS who was shot by one of the military on St. Mary's Bridge in the excitement of the contested election of a member of Parliament for this town 20th November 1868 when the constitutional battle for religious equality was fought and won.

On the reverse side: Erected by subscription AD.1869.

(437)

The Cross which was erected by Public Subscription to James Woods who was shot by the Military in 1868.

WOODS
Erected by Patrick Woods of Drogheda, Manufacturer, in memory of his son James Woods who departed this life 20th October 1804 aged 8 years.

(723)

WOODS
See Gargan.

(218)

WOOGAN
Erected by John Woogan of Old Hill, Drogheda, in memory of Patrick Boyle late of the Dale who died 7th July 1869 and his wife Mary Boyle who died October 1846. Also their children Patrick Laurence and Mary who died young. His wife Julia Woogan who died 18th May 1874 aged 64 years.

(750)

Entrance to The Cord in Thomas Street.

The Cord Cemetery